Invisible Tears

THE ABUSE THE REBELLION THE SURVIVAL
DESPITE ALL ODDS

Abigail Lawrence

authorHOUSE®

AuthorHouse™ UK Ltd.
500 Avebury Boulevard
Central Milton Keynes, MK9 2BE
www.authorhouse.co.uk
Phone: 08001974150

Registered with the IP Rights Office
Copyright Registration Service
Ref: 1012157921

© 2010 Abigail Lawrence. All rights reserved.

No part of this book may be reproduced, stored in a retrieval system, or transmitted by any means without the written permission of the author.

First published by AuthorHouse   3/30/2010

ISBN: 978-1-4490-7002-1 (sc)

This work is a memoir and is based on a true story. It reflects the author's present recollection of her experiences over a period of years. Certain names, locations and identifying characteristics have been changed to protect people, and certain individuals are composites. Dialogue and events have been recreated from memory and in some cases compressed to convey the substance of what was said or what occurred.

Every effort was made to corroborate memory with fact. All of which is not to say that every word of this book is true it has been added to and a lot is hearsay. Some sequences and details of events have been changed — that said, most human stories are subject to errors of omission, fact, or interpretation regardless of intent.

Edited by Steven Ward

This book is printed on acid-free paper.

Dedicated to my wonderful family
and my amazing husband.

Chapter 1

12 November 1972

"Sshhh, they'll hear you!" An unfamiliar, female voice sounded angry as it wafted up the steps. There was a lot of whispering downstairs. I had no idea who she was, but from the edge in her voice, I knew she was frustrated.

They probably thought we couldn't hear if they whispered, because we were supposed to be in our rooms not on the landing. Thirty or forty of them were crammed into our little two up two down semi-detached council house.

I had no idea who these people were but they were dressed smartly. Most were wearing suits, some with flared trousers and long collars on flowery shirts, all very fashionable back in the 70's. There weren't any children so I figured the party was for adults only.

"What about the kids?" The same female voice rose above the rest.

What kids? I wondered. She had a funny accent; it sang with tones going up and down the scales, a bit like Welsh or

Irish. There was urgency in her voice that made me feel sorry for those unfortunate "kids" she was talking about.

The familiar smell of tobacco floated upstairs. I loved that smell. It was mummy's boyfriend who always smoked a pipe. He had been living here and taking care of us while mummy had been in hospital. I didn't hear his voice, just smelt him, so I knew he was there. I closed my eyes and breathed in that delicious aroma of cherry tobacco which permeated everything in the room.

The party seemed in full flow downstairs with lots of food laid on and gentle music from Bobby Darin playing in the background. Mummy always liked his singing. She had most of his records and would often pick me up and swing me around while singing and dancing away to his songs.

I was really annoyed we had to stay upstairs. *Who are all these people, anyway? Anyone I know?* I felt like I was missing out on the fun, hiding up here in my fluffy romper-suit pyjamas. I hoped we wouldn't get caught as we strained to see between the banisters.

The brown and orange patterned wallpaper distracted me for a moment. I tried to remember how many patterns I had counted one night when I was sent to bed early. The loose bit of wallpaper low to the skirting board was too much to resist so I couldn't fight the urge. I had to pick away at it. The carpet was orange too, with a green swirly pattern going through. It was thick and fluffy and felt lovely between my toes. The curtains matched the green shades in the carpet but had a different pattern. I hated those curtains because they looked like someone vomited.

"It's not fair. Why don't us kids ever get to go to the parties?" I asked my brother, Alex.

"Shut up Abbie," he chided. He was sulking too.

Alex was eight, two years older than me, but he acted much older. The only other member of my immediate family was Pepsi, our black, pet miniature poodle. She was being a pain as usual, constantly bringing me her toy to throw and yipping until I did. I threw it into the bedroom in a hurry, because if the adults heard her, we'd be in trouble.

"Shhhh. Pepsi. I can't hear."

That same female voice shouted angrily, "Then they'll have to come with me, for now."

An older man's voice butted in, "They'll go into a kid's home over my dead body! They're coming with me. And, by the way, where the hell is their father?"

Good point, I thought. *Where the hell is my daddy? Haven't seen him for weeks.* I wouldn't have minded but he was only around the corner until a little while ago, and then he just disappeared. I heard someone say he had shacked up with mummy's friend one street away. Alex and I had promised not to tell mummy, but we used to go and visit daddy there while we were playing with his friend's kids. Molly, Debbie and Daniel were our friends, but now they had disappeared too.

I had a really bad feeling in my tummy all day. I didn't know why, but I felt kind of sick and scared.

When the adults argued, Alex started crying and ran to his bedroom. He never liked anyone to see him cry.

I couldn't help but wonder who was going to look after me and my brother. I let go of the banister and ran after Alex to see what was wrong.

He turned and asked, "Do you think she's dead?" He looked quite concerned with tears in his eyes.

"It's no good asking me," I shrugged. What on earth was he going on about? He was trying to talk to me, but it was difficult to understand him between sobs and gasps. I went back on the landing and strained to hear exactly what was going on. Then I ran back to Alex's room.

"Who's dead, Alex? Who?" I was totally clueless while I stood in the doorway. I tried to listen to the soft voices from there but it was no use. "What does dead mean?" I knew mummy had been ill because we had visited her in hospital.

She told me I was her "Princess." "Mummy loves you," I could still hear her say the words as her boyfriend took us out of the room. We never got to go back and see her again because we had been sent to spend a few nights with some friends. I guess I'd never realised how ill she was.

"It means she's d-e-a-d, dead, stupid. She's never, ever coming back." Alex snapped.

"Who, Alex?" I was getting annoyed.

The enormity of what he said slammed my brain when the realisation finally hit home. I remember that scream inside my head, like it was yesterday. I'm not sure if the noise came out, but it was like a never ending wail. "Muuummy?" *Does he mean Mummy?* I panicked. I cried so hard I couldn't even see through my tears.

I shouted over and over, "Mummy! Mummy!" throwing myself on the floor in a crumpled heap. I grabbed the banisters and cried, "Mummy!" through the bars.

A lady came running up the stairs and pried my fingers from the bars. She pulled me away from the banisters and hugged me so tight. I didn't know her name but I didn't want her to let go.

"It will be okay, sweetheart," she said in a calm and caring way. "It will be okay." She stroked my hair and held me to her breast while my tears and dribble soaked her dark blue flowery dress. She didn't seem to mind. Wiping my runny nose on my pyjama sleeve, I saw Pepsi bring me her toy. She stood there waiting and tilting her head side to side, listening as she pawed at her toy. At first I thought she was trying to cheer me up, but as usual, she just wanted to play.

It was then that I realized the kids all the people downstairs were talking about were us, me and Alex. *Oh my,* I thought, *Mummy's been buried and the wake is at our house.*

It was a dark and scary journey through the night, and it seemed to go on forever. Travelling from Norfolk to somewhere up north in the early 70's was torture for a six-year-old, but losing my mother made me numb. All the way to Uncle Trevor's house we sat in silence, not speaking for the entire journey. *What do you say to complete strangers?* I wondered. That's who the people in the front of the car were to me, until they introduced themselves as relatives. We also didn't have a clue where they were taking us.

We arrived at Uncle Trevor's house somewhere in Manchester. I was relieved they had kids of their own. I will never forget walking into their living room. After all these years, it seems like yesterday. It looked very cosy and had a coal fire which lit the entire room with a warm orange glow. I could feel the heat from it standing in the doorway, but I thought it smelt awful. The smoke stayed in my throat when I breathed. *I'd rather have our old electric heater,* I thought. *It didn't smell so bad.*

I looked across the room and saw four kids, one boy, all of them wearing white night-dresses. I thought, *That's weird*, and smiled and giggled to myself. We were offered a cup of Horlicks as the kids welcomed us into their home.

We lived with them for several weeks. I have no real memories of the time we spent with them but I'm sure they were kind to us. Actually I'm not sure how long it was before daddy came. It's all a distant blur.

People were saying our daddy had "buggered off," not giving a toss about his kids. I didn't believe a word because daddy would never leave us. These people obviously didn't know my daddy, or they were from mummy's side. Otherwise, they wouldn't be saying stuff like that.

One day his long awaited arrival was announced with a shout at my Uncle, "They are my kids and there is nothing you can do about it!"

I had the urge to run up and hug him because I hadn't seen my daddy for ages. But they both looked mad and the arguing held me back. I heard daddy explain that he had remarried and, as it later turned out, to my mummy's friend, the one who lived one street away. She was the one who we had agreed to keep secret.

"You try and stop me!" Daddy warned.

The next thing I knew I was sitting in the back of his old Austin. I could smell the exhaust fumes coming in the back while I watched the world go by. Little did I know we were going to live with him and his new family, forever. Somehow, even though things were tough, knowing we were going to live with our old friends that had disappeared was really exciting. I waddled in a cradle of naivety. *Daddy loves me,* I thought. *He came back, didn't he?*

I sat in the car feeling scared again. *Where are we going?* I was chuffed to bits that daddy finally found us, even if it had taken awhile. I lost my mummy, but at least I had my daddy back.

Alex was always the "daddy's boy," and he was so happy for the first time in what seemed like years. But of course, it had only been weeks. *Whatever happened to Pepsi?* I wondered. *She just disappeared a bit like we did.* I asked daddy where Pepsi was several times, but it only annoyed him.

"We have a new dog now," daddy said sounding impatient. "It's a Rough-Collie called Sunny."

"I want Pepsi," I said. "She's my dog." All of a sudden I was in tears again. *Where is Pepsi?* I wondered. *Where is my dog, mummy's dog?*

I thought daddy coming to get us would make everything all right again. I was so pleased to see him, nothing else should have mattered, but Pepsi was the only thing I remembered that mummy had loved.

I didn't know why, but my tummy had a bad feeling.

Chapter 2

Molly, Debbie and Daniel were there waiting to greet us. An exciting five minutes was followed by the arrival of daddy's new wife, Sue. She said, "Hello," gave a quick hug without even looking at us and then pushed us aside to get to daddy. I didn't know where to look when I saw her kissing him with an open mouth. She looked like a Vampire trying to eat his lips. *That's my daddy,* I thought. *Keep your hands off! Who are you anyway?* Her own kids were told to go clean up the kitchen whilst Sue showed us up to our rooms.

I remembered Sue from when she was my mummy's friend. She was a very pretty woman and she knew it with plenty of male attention. She had long legs always shown off by the shortest of miniskirts. Her breasts although large were nicely shaped by some kind of special bras, pushed together like a couple of balloons, always showing lots of cleavage. She maintained a full face of make-up. In fact, she seemed to wake up with make up on, never going downstairs until she looked pretty, and with perfectly polished finger nails too, always red and perfect. Her dark brown hair was permed into tight curls--afro's were the fashion. She had big blue, drilling eyes. When she stared at me, I had to look away. Straight away I knew I had to respect this lady; everyone did and nobody argued with her. *She's always right you know!*

I was sharing with two girls, Debbie aged eight and Molly six. We had bunk beds and there weren't any blankets, just sheets.

"You don't need blankets," Sue stated in a matter of fact way. "It gets far too hot in this house."

I looked for toys and thought to myself, *That's a good point, where are my toys?* The bedroom looked out into a small garden. *Maybe my toys are outside or in daddy's car? Guess I'll have to wait until tomorrow, when it's light.*

Alex wasn't too happy about sharing a room with Daniel, he was only three. Debbie was the oldest. She made it very clear she didn't want us there and certainly didn't want to share her mum. She hardly said a word to me but seemed to get on well with Alex, maybe because her birthday was three days before his and it was like they were twins.

Debbie looked like her mum with the most beautiful long, dark hair. It was almost black and with her tanned skin she looked very healthy. But there was something dark and evil behind those eyes that hinted of misery.

Molly was totally different, she was very plain and pale skinned, skinny and not at all pretty. She had teeth protruding all over the place and looked like a good candidate for a brace. But she was a lovely person, always sweet, and we seemed to get on so well right from the start. She was only two months older than me and we often pretended we were twins too.

Things seemed fine for a few days. We were shown around the local area by the kids. We saw the school we would be going to and went shopping for school uniforms.

Daddy came into our bedroom early the next morning. He woke me up and gently whispered, "Honey I've got to go back to work. I will see you next week."

I thought I was dreaming until I woke up a short while later and daddy was gone. I was brushing my teeth when a pain shot right through the side of my head.

Next thing I knew Sue was screaming at me, "I called you, you little bitch and when I call you, you had better move!" The pain I felt was her right hand slapping me round the head, the force enough to knock me off my feet.

"Get downstairs," she screamed right in my face. I had never been hit before, I was shocked. My brain froze in shear panic. I ran downstairs with all the kids looking at me.

Alex asked, "What's wrong Abbie?"

"Butt out!" she shouted, "or you'll soon find out."

The others ignored what was happening and carried on with what they were doing. They obviously knew better than to cross Sue.

"Sit down here," she smirked pointing to the floor in front of her feet. "That is just a taster of what you'll get the next time you ignore me."

I sat down and noticed her toes were painted red too. "I didn't ignore you Sue," I pleaded. The next thing I knew my hair felt like it was being pulled out in chunks as I was dragged across the floor,

"Don't you dare," she growled. She was so angry with me and I didn't know why. "Don't you dare answer me back. Now get up," she bellowed, her face contorting. She didn't look pretty anymore.

I scrambled to my feet.

"Quicker," she said, just as my head was wacked off the nearest wall. "I'll knock some sense into you, you spoilt little "daddy's girl." She spat in my face, she was so close I was afraid she was going to bite me. Pain was soaring through my head, and I felt sick and dizzy. She continued screaming, "I am your mother now and you'd better shape up girl. Your own mother found a way to get away from you. I don't blame her either, you ugly little shit, don't you EVER call me SUE again. Understand?"

"Please, please," I begged her over and over, but she wouldn't leave me alone. It just seemed to make her want to hurt me more.

"From now on you call me Mum and think yourself lucky I took you in, because no one else wants you."

No one else wants you, no one else want you. Those words stuck with me like a dagger to the heart. *No one wants me?* I was devastated.

That was the first time we were left alone with her. She didn't even give us a chance to settle in before the beatings started. I remember being kept off school for a few days. I had to stay in bed locked in my room with my bucket to pee in. My head hurt so much I couldn't move without being sick, and I kept seeing dots floating around my room. I felt dizzy all the time.

"How long has she been like this?" daddy asked her on his return the following weekend. Daddy was a truck driver and worked abroad all week, just coming home on weekends, which left our new "mum" free to do whatever she wanted.

"She fell down the stairs," Sue lied, barking at him.

"Fell down?" he said looking me over. I wanted to scream but I was afraid.

"Don't you dare judge me, I am not your babysitter. Besides she has been a brat all week, and I've had to get tough with her too. I can't cope with five kids especially if she is going to be a brat."

Daddy looked at the bruises on my face. I could see the pain in his eyes, but he said nothing and walked away. Right from the start I thought he knew I had done nothing, but he didn't say a word. If I spoke up, I was afraid she might kill me.

Monday morning soon came, and daddy woke me up again. He said, "Be a good girl, Princess and I will be back at the weekend." Panic immediately set in; I lay in bed and held on to him.

"Don't go Daddy… please don't go." I tried to hang on but he pushed me away. I cried out after him. I really wanted to tell him what she had done and what I was frightened she would do again, but I couldn't. He must have seen the fear in my eyes.

"Shhh," he said with his soothing voice. "Things will be okay, just be a good girl for me." He walked back, kissed me on the cheek and off he went for another week.

I heard the door close downstairs and dad's car start. It pulled off down the road, then footsteps headed toward our room. I pulled the sheet over my head not wanting her to know I was awake but it was too late. She stomped in, grabbed my hair and dragged me out of bed. Out on the landing, she screamed in a sarcastic taking-the-pee tone of voice, "Aaaw daddy's princess is sad. Aaaw poor little girl being left here all alone. What are you trying to do, make your daddy cross with me or something?"

"No," I cried. I should have known better because it fell on deaf ears. "I miss my daddy…I want my daddy!"

I sobbed, but laughter filled the air. She was too busy laughing at me to hear me cry. A cane stood propped just outside the door. I was sure it hadn't been there before. She grabbed it as she passed and told me to bend over,

"No… no… no!" I begged holding onto myself, covering my bottom from her with my hands.

"Each time you say no, you will get more," she added and laughed while grabbing my hands away, "Go on, keep saying no," She warned as she ripped my nightdress off leaving me stood almost naked in just my knickers. She told me, "You get yourself in my bedroom, bend over the end of that bed and grab hold of the bed frame.

To this day it sends chills up my spine. I'll never forget the coldness of that chrome. "If you let go of the bed I will keep doing it," she shouted at me. Her eyes looked like they would bulge out of her head. Those enormous eyes had such anger in them. The first smack hurt badly but obviously not enough, so she pulled down my knickers and started hitting me harder. The pain was unreal and I thought, *Why? Why is this happening to me? What did I do?* She counted to twenty then stopped and left me crumpled in a fetal heap on the floor of her bedroom, shaking and sobbing. *Why?*

She left the room. "Hurry up and get ready for school," she shouted up the stairs.

My teacher looked at me sometimes like she knew what was happening. I had tried to tell a teacher several times but the thought of what I'd get from mum for telling tales would be worse, so I didn't bother. Besides the whole nightmare was too embarrassing to tell anyone.

I often heard Alex crying and shouting. One morning I woke to piercing screams, "No, please no more, please stop Mum." I had been dreaming, then shook my head to realise what I heard was not in my dream. I ran to his room and stopped still frozen, standing in the doorway. I looked over to where mum was stood over him, hitting him over and over again because his bed was wet. Alex had started bed-wetting after my real mummy died.

"I'm sorry," he cried "I won't do it again." He pleaded with her as she grabbed him and shoved his face into the wet sheets, rubbing his head around in the urine. She shouted at him constantly telling him how dirty he was. I tip-toed back to my room before she saw me. What could I do? But I could still hear her.

"If you like to be wet that much, then you can smell like it all day," she said to Alex in front of Daniel. I had seen Daniel huddled up on his bed looking terrified.

And so it was; Alex had to go to school smelling of wee most days. Luckily none of his friends noticed or if they did, no one ever said anything. On return home from school every day when he had been wet the night before, he would be made to go into the bathroom and wash his sheets in the bath, sometimes with bleach if they had stained. One night he had to sleep on the floor with no covers as his bed sheets weren't dry. That became a regular thing; most nights he slept on the floor.

It wasn't long after that I began to realise I couldn't stand hearing him scream any longer. To this day I don't know what came over me; maybe it was his wailing that went straight through me like a sharp knife through warm butter. One night I ran into his bedroom and threw myself over him to protect my big brother.

"Leave him alone," I shouted mustering up all my courage.

That was the start of me standing up for Alex. But, of course, I also took a lot of his punishment, or got punished right along-side. At six-years-old I learnt it was easier to be beaten than to witness my brother screaming like that. It was just the way I was.

Alex didn't stop wetting his bed. He wouldn't tell mum it was wet and would just sleep in it for days until she found out.

The rooms never got too cold for blankets. It was freezing to me. We often got into each other's beds and cuddled up to keep warm.

We lived in a small town near Coventry. It was a quiet street with houses that all looked the same, the same red brick with the same porches. They all had bin sheds by the front door that were painted different colours, ours was red. It was a typical town council estate, but not far away was wide open country. I loved wandering out in the country. We got to know the area well, like where the best places were to go fruit picking or scrumping and where to get the best blackberries and gooseberries. At weekends we were kicked out of the house after breakfast--that's if we were lucky enough to get any--and told not to return until after tea time. We were not allowed back in the house under any circumstances, rain or snow. We couldn't even use the toilet and certainly not allowed lunch. If we needed the loo then a bush would have to do. There were enough of us to be lookouts and watch for people coming. So we pretty much did as we liked and went where we liked. It was so wonderful just being away from her.

I was probably about seven years old when I found my love of horses. It was during one of those cold, wet days where we had to entertain ourselves. There was a beautiful grey horse nearby. I used to stop and stroke it whenever I went by and give it an apple I'd stolen scrumping from a neighbour's tree. It was so friendly. One day after watching cowboys on television I decided I'd see if I could ride it, going against Molly's pleas and begging me not to. I don't know what possessed me but I climbed up the fence and dragged myself onto the horse's back. I had never sat on a horse before, never mind actually riding one. I didn't have a clue what to do but I'd seen in Westerns on TV that you kick them, so that's what I did.

My heart was beating like crazy; the horse galloped down its field and jumped the paddock fence. It then started running around all the gardens in that posh housing estate. Whilst Molly watched with her mouth gaping open in shock, I couldn't control it. I was just a passenger on a huge grey cloud. I could feel its breathing under me and the power it had as it moved and I grabbed onto it's mane to keep me aboard.

Although I was struck dumb by the beauty of that horse, I knew I would be in serious trouble for this one. So when it stopped to eat grass I slid off its back leaving it to fend for itself in some person's landscaped garden, hoof prints everywhere. How I didn't fall off and break my neck I will never know. I ran away from the evidence giggling inside and buzzing from excitement. As I caught up with Molly we ran away from the scene of the crime together and were looking back over our shoulders to see whether any curtains were moving. *Had anyone seen me?* The post lady pulled up emptying the mailbox, and we breathed a sigh of relief that she hadn't turned up two minutes earlier and witnessed the destruction.

No one had seen me, only my step-sister Molly.

"You will be in major trouble now," she said with a shocked expression all over her face. "But, don't worry, I won't tell." She smiled at me, her brown eyes sparkling. All the way home we were giggling and remembering how that horse had jumped out of its paddock with me clinging on for dear life.

"I was a little scared," I said.

"You looked like you were flying," Molly squealed,

"I felt like I it too," I bragged. I wasn't going to let on how frightened I really was. I didn't for a minute think of the danger I had put myself or that poor horse into. All I could think about was hoping and praying Sue didn't find out. I was glad it was just Molly and me; I couldn't trust the others.

Sue never did hear of it. That horse gave me a valuable gift, a sense of power just for a snapshot in time. The thrill of that ride let me escape my misery and go somewhere else. That was the dream I hung onto and often brought back to life. I remembered it whilst I was getting beaten on a regular basis. I would hold onto the chrome bed and think of that horse. I'd travel away, miles and miles away from reality; that way the cane didn't hurt so much. Memories of that ride, a brief moment of ecstasy, would serve me well.

Chapter 3

The force of the slipper hitting the side of my head and face stung like a million bees. Mum's pink slippers were the ones that had fluffy feathers on the front, with a small, hard heal. She always looked good even in her slippers. I fell to floor crumpled up into as tight a ball as I could make. Well trained, I knew how to "assume the position." When I balled up it hurt less when she hit me over and over again.

"Who do you think you are, you lazy cow? Everyone else is doing their fair share of housework, but no, not you." Her voice wailed at me. Like the sound of a knife scraping a plate, it went right through to my spinal cord.

"I don't feel well, honest mum," I said. My stomach churned, the shooting pains running around my tummy like little knives cutting me up. Then, at that exact moment, I hurled right where I was sat on the carpet, my stomach cramping. I grabbed it holding on and squeezing myself while trying to crawl to the toilet, the pains still shooting in all directions. I grabbed my mouth to try and stop being sick again. The next blow to my head sent me flying, projecting vomit everywhere like a loose garden hose. She grabbed me by the hair and dragged me back into the room, rubbing my face in the mess on the carpet.

"Eat it you dirty little slag," she screamed. "Clean it up, lick it, go on, it's only fair after your brothers and sisters have spent all morning cleaning while you were hiding away." She rubbed my face down hard, pushing it into the carpet. I thought I felt my nose crack and it started bleeding.

She went on, "Is this how much you appreciate them? Bleed all over it too, why don't you?" The taste of carpet fibre and puke made me vomit, and each time she shoved my face in and made me lick it up, I was sick again. My stomach wasn't letting up; I felt cold, sweaty and had goose bumps all over. I could taste blood running down the back of my throat. *How can this be happening?* I thought. *Where are the other kids?* No one ever tried to stop her from hurting me. Not like me, I always tried to help my brothers and sisters. Eventually she got bored with the whole mess and walked away. Not even looking at me, she discharged me with a point of her finger toward the stairs. I ran.

I spent the rest of the day in bed locked in my room. I had a bucket to use as a toilet and to be sick in. I heard the front door slam, a key in the lock and footsteps walking away. Her high-heel s made sharp clicks. *She's gone,* I thought. *I can finally relax.*

The sound of the birds outside and the hum of a lawn mower played a song in the back of my mind. My head throbbed, my face stung from the carpet burns and my lip was black, fat and swollen. Every now and then I could taste blood, and my nose was far too sore to touch. Those sounds from outside sent me off to sleep, all day I drifted in and out. As I woke up after a while I could hear neighbours in the garden talking. "Those poor kids." and "Someone has got to do something, surely." I hoped and prayed they would, but no one ever did. No one interfered back in those days. Beating children was quite common.

The school had been given a letter saying I fell down the stairs whilst playing magic carpets. My teacher looked at me and smiled sweetly showing off her white, straight teeth. I moved my tongue around my mouth feeling the gap where my two front teeth were missing.

She said, "Well you should be more careful young lady." Then she went on with her business.

I felt that she knew, the frown lines in her forehead and wayward glance, not making eye contact when she spoke gave it away. *She knows. The neighbours know. Why?* I wondered. *Why doesn't someone come to help us?* People just looked the other way.

It became routine that we had to do all the housework before school. Mum would sit and paint her nails while barking orders. The work was always done in silence with everyone trying so hard to get it right the first time. Sometimes we managed, but if she had to move off the sofa or correct you, a slipper or an object that was close at hand, a ballistic missile would come hurtling with deadly accuracy towards your head. And that was if you were lucky and her nails were wet. Woe betide you if the nails were dry!

Mondays were the worst. It was almost like she had to behave so well when daddy was home and use so much self-control, she had to make up for it when he left. It was lovely when daddy was around; everyone laughed and joked. Daddy loved music and would sit on a Sunday afternoon recording the top twenty charts on the radio. We would all dance around pretending to be at a disco. While singing, "*Tie a yellow ribbon round the old Oak tree,*" I thought, *How nice it would be if he was here all the time.*

"Daddy please don't go to work this week!" we would all plead, but he always went to work leaving us to it, and things very quickly got back to normal.

I couldn't help screaming, the thought of having my fingers cut off was too much. "I promise, I promise I will stop biting my nails," I said, petrified as usual and begging her to stop.

She held my fingers down on the thick wooden chopping board with a carving knife pressing into the tops of my fingers near the knuckles, keeping them tight onto the board. I could feel the cold blade splitting my skin as mum slowly slid the knife back and forth over my fingers scraping and cutting at the skin.

"Oh mum, it hurts!" I cried.

"You will never have nails like mine," she said digging her nails deep into my hand leaving indentations that would stay there for at least an hour as a reminder.

"Your nails are disgusting! I might just as well chop them off," she teased, enjoying every moment of my horror. She clouted me around the ear and told me to, "Bugger off." If she ever caught me biting my nails, out would come the chopping board. She often whacked my fingers with a rolling pin or whatever was close to hand if the knife wasn't handy.

I'm sure she got pleasure out of my tears, but the more time that went by the harder it was to make me cry. Most of the time I just pretended to cry because I knew what she wanted. The quicker I cried, the quicker she would leave me alone. If I didn't cry she became angrier and angrier; she would hit harder or find new weapons or creative ways of inflicting pain.

I started to dread watching TV at night, because sometimes when the others were having a bath or had been sent to their rooms, she would make me lie across the sofa with my head on her lap. I had to lie on my tummy with my face buried in her lap. I hated the smell down there, but she would push my head in harder and harder, holding and pushing the back of my head. I would choke and gag for breath, then she would let me breathe before pushing my head in again. I couldn't figure why but this seemed to make her happy. After a while I knew she would let me breathe. I would pretend to panic and gag quicker, so she would let me up for air before I would panic for real. She'd go on and on then moan and sigh and tell me I was a good girl.

Food was scarce for the kids in our house. She would cook lovely meals for herself or any one of our Uncles, but all us kid's were fed separately, horrible food. If I complained she would force the tripe into my mouth and make me choke.

"It's good for you," she'd laugh, "If you don't eat it today, it will be there tomorrow."

It was too. Days would go by where the very same plate of food would be put in front of me. I suppose I was saved by the other kids sneaking bits of food off their plates for me. Only when it got to the weekend and dad was home did it stop. But, I would pay for it on Monday morning when he left again. She never forgot.

Alex got away with quite a lot more as time went on. I would take the blame for things he did and he would sneak nice food to my room as a trade-off. The other kids would take their fair share of beatings too, everyone except Debbie. Debbie was the spoilt one. Whilst we would have charity shop or jumble clothes, Debbie had nice new clothes to go with her long shiny hair, brown eyes and olive dark skin. She looked very exotic. We all wanted to look like Debbie.

Molly constantly had her head banged off the wall. "I will knock some sense into you if it kills me," mum would scream while smashing her head into the wall. Holding on to her hair either side, mum gripped her head with perfectly manicured hands. Molly was a bit simple, they all said. The kid's at school picked on her too no matter how hard she worked at pleasing them. Mum often tried to knock some sense into her.

Dad started staying away at work some weekends. That meant that there was no escape from mum's mood swings. We would be up and out of the house by eight in the morning and not allowed back until teatime whatever the weather. Sometimes we would go out in shorts and t-shirts and as the weather changed and maybe rained all day, we would freeze and shiver. If we tried to get back in, we were told, "Tough," or "Bugger off!" There were times when we would huddle up in the ally beside our house to try and stay warm.

After we cleaned up the house daily, very often we would be locked in our rooms with just our bucket. Mum would go out and leave us alone and locked in. That happened on lots of occasions where mum would go out with one of her male friends. She was trying to get on TV you know and was seeing lots of different men from that circle of friends who could help her. They were friends that were hers and not daddy's. Men friends who daddy never even met started to come around a lot.

Chapter 4

I was nine years old when I was told by mum, "Go and take this envelope around Uncle Joe's house." It was just after breakfast and she said, "I have to pay him for the favour he did with the lawn cutting, and you're the one he wants to bring it for some reason," she smirked and looked very pleased with herself.

He lived about a 45 minute walk over in the posh area. I had never walked that far by myself and I was a little nervous about losing my way. I loved looking at the posh houses with the smart, tidy front gardens full of flowers and nice cars parked in the driveways. It looked like only happy families lived there.

Uncle Joe was nice to us kids when he came round our house, often giving us a wink and a boiled sweet from his pocket. We would sit on his lap for stories while he waited for mum to get ready to go out with him. It always took a long time for her to get ready, and she always looked so pretty when she went out. She had to impress the TV people or she would never get on TV shows. Dad knew she wanted to get onto the TV, but I don't think he knew how often she went out. We would be locked in our bedrooms with our buckets to pee in. It didn't matter what time she went out and sometimes she didn't come back until early the following morning.

I never felt uncomfortable when Joe picked me up and put me on his lap. At first I would shift around a lot but I would get a warning glance from mum if she walked in. She would say, "Stop wriggling around and sit still." So I sat still, even when his hand would accidently on purpose slide up my thigh between my legs while he adjusted me on his lap. He was never nasty to me though. In fact he was so nice and kind that mum would say he had a soft spot for me. All the men did, she said, but she didn't know why.

"You are so ugly! What a blessing your real mum died. She would've died of shock if she could see how ugly you are growing up to be."

Sometimes if no one was in the room with us, Uncle Joe kept his fingers there, between my legs, moving them gently back and forth, stroking my private bits over the top of my knickers. He was so gentle and it was quite comforting, especially if mum had given me a good hiding that day. I thought it was nice that someone showed me some kind of affection. He was always gentle and kind to us girls.

I didn't know it was wrong for him to do that. After a while, none of us would want to sit on his lap, it made us feel weird. Mum would pick one of us up and plonk us on one of her friend's lap and tell him to read us a story. I tried to stay still like she said, but some of the men did fidget a lot.

I remember being jealous because when Debbie or Molly had been messenger for mum, she was so pleased with them. They were treated nicely and got to stay up late and watch TV eating sweets or crisps. "You're a good girl," she would say. "You're helping Mum get on TV being my messenger, and when I get on TV we will be rich and get to live in a posh house too."

I couldn't figure out how us going to and from Uncle Joe's house giving messages was going to help her get onto

TV, but we certainly were not going to argue. No one argued with mum.

Walking up that posh road, as mum's messenger for the first time, I knew she would be pleased with me. *Will I get sweets and TV tonight?* I wondered. After all, it was a long walk and I would be as good a messenger as any.

"Give him the letter and do exactly as you're told," she warned as I was leaving, "Don't you annoy him in any way. And if you spoil my chances of getting on TV you will feel my wrath like you've never felt it before girl." Why would I annoy Uncle Joe? He was one of the few people who was actually nice to me.

Uncle Joe's house was especially posh. It had blue shutters by the windows and a playhouse in the garden. I didn't know if he had kids; I had never seen any. Maybe he was divorced? Joe came smiling to the door open-armed ready to pick me up. He seemed so very pleased to see me.

"And how's my favourite little Princess," he said greeting me with a huge hug. I smiled remembering daddy called me that too, and I walked inside handing him the letter. Uncle Joe wasn't a big man, quite small really, even smaller than daddy. He had reddish hair and ginger eyebrows. He had a small beard and a small moustache. Lines on his face around his mouth and eyes crinkled when he smiled and he had dimples on his cheeks. He read the letter quickly then turned to speak to me.

"I was just about to watch a film on TV," he said pointing to the television. "Do you want to stay and watch it with me? The letter says you're allowed to stay for tea."

"Oh yes," I beamed with joy. I couldn't believe my luck. I would have been even more jealous of Debbie and Molly, if I knew they got this kind of treatment. I was so happy I'd been allowed to go this time.

"Come on then," he beckoned. "Let's get comfy." He pulled me onto his lap for a cuddle as he normally did. I was more than happy to sit on his lap while stuffing my face with milk and biscuits. It was pure heaven. Looking around I saw lots of pictures of children. *Maybe he does have kids.*

I was sat on his lap for a while when he adjusted me further pulling me right in close. He started petting my leg, then his hand moved all the way up my thigh to my knickers and again he started stroking my privates. I don't know how long he did it, as I was so engrossed watching the film on TV. I had forgotten he was touching me at all, until another adjustment and his fingers slid into my knickers gently touching and rubbing my bare private bits with his thumb. It felt strange as he had never moved my knickers before. I tensed and started to shift nervously, trying to pull away and get down. But he would have none of it. He pulled me close again and held me tightly with enough force to make me think about what mum said, "Don't annoy him." So I said nothing and tried to be still.

"You are such an angel," he said. I could feel his breath on my neck and his whiskers tickled. "Your Mum told me you are old enough to play grown up games now."

Games mean fun, I thought. So I turned and smiled and said, "If mum said I can, then I guess it's okay." I was pleased she thought I was old enough to play grown up games. *What are grown up games?* I wondered. I hoped she would be kind to me that night.

I could feel a hard lump in Uncle Joe's trousers. His bottom bits seemed to be throbbing. Uncle Joe moved me aside then stood up and went out of the room for a minute, returning with a camera.

"Get undressed," he said in a matter-of-fact way, like it was nothing at all. "Take your dress off," he repeated a little louder when I didn't move straight away. I shifted slowly towards the edge of the sofa then stood up. I must have looked concerned because Uncle Joe got very angry and snapped at me.

"Okay don't! I will just write a letter back to your Mum and you can be on your way," he said while standing up and moving towards the door.

"No, no it's okay." I panicked at the thought. If mum found out, I would be in for a beating. Nothing could be worse than that cane. I quickly took off my blue cotton, gingham summer dress and that left me stood there in my vest and white cotton knickers. I could feel the heat rise in my face with the blood rushing to make it so obvious that I was embarrassed. I wrapped my arms around myself, shivering, but I wasn't cold.

"Now lie down on the floor and open your legs," he demanded, pointing to where he wanted me. I did as I was told, laying down slowly not knowing what to put where. I felt like a plastic doll as if my body couldn't bend. At that point he grabbed my knees and pushed open my legs and told me to stay still. I'm not sure how long he took photographs of me, but it wasn't that bad. *Why he would want such silly pictures?* I wondered. After a while he pulled my vest off, leaving me with naked nipples and skin crawling with goose bumps. Now I was scared!

"You can get dressed now," he said smiling. "You've been a very good girl and I will write and tell your Mum so."

I did get to stay up that night. Mum was very pleased with me, and it felt so nice to feel good around her for once. She was like a different person.

"You made me proud ," she smiled handing me crisps and a bar of chocolate. Later, I heard her on the telephone saying, "I was quite pleased with Abbie. She could become my most valuable possession."

For the first time in a long time, I had a sense of belonging and a feeling that I was actually wanted.

Chapter 5

"Sit down kids, we have some news for you," daddy said.

Mum and dad stood together in the living room; they were very happy about something. We were all jumping around when mum said, "We have a new baby on the way." She sounded like the sweetest person, not the person I knew.

"That will make six of us," Alex said. We giggled.

"You all have to make a big effort to help mum around the house now," daddy said.

What? Mum never lifted a finger before she got pregnant, I thought, *What makes him think she will now?* She threw a glare in my direction. *Surely I didn't say that out loud?* I kept my fingers crossed I hadn't. Then again, the witch could probably read my mind.

The baby was beautiful. I don't remember ever being allowed to hold her though. Her name was Kassie, and she was the most perfect thing I had ever seen.

Dad was home for awhile when Kassie was born, so of course things seemed really nice, lots of laughter and fun. We went on holiday to Butlins too. It was a great time, even though we had to stay in our chalet room at night while mum and dad went out. We still loved every minute of it, and, for a while, the beatings stopped.

It didn't take too long to get back to normal. When dad went back to work, the torture got even worse. I was getting beaten most every day for something. Her latest weapon of choice was a belt.

"Don't draw on the walls," she shouted as she belted my legs and backside. Dad had lots of belts with different buckles. He liked Cowboy and Western films, so the buckles on his belts were big and hurt a lot more than ordinary buckles. This time I had to choose which belt I wanted. I hadn't drawn on the walls. Daniel had, but what was the point in arguing? I just assumed the position.

Later that day, I was told that Uncle Joe wanted to see me. My visits there were getting more and more frequent. Most of the time he would take pictures or fiddle with my bits, but I didn't mind as he was very nice to me. I was getting used to posing for the camera too.

"Your Mum tells me you've had the belt today?" he questioned when I arrived at his house. I sat gingerly on the edge of the sofa nursing my raw bottom.

"Yes I have," I nodded sadly. Uncle Joe liked to see where mum had spanked me. He would take photographs of my bottom and my marked back. He said he wanted to show his friends how cruel she was. He would kiss my bottom better and rub cream on it. I never saw the pot of cream but when I was lying on my tummy he always squirted me with warm cream and rubbed it in to make it better. It did feel quite soothing.

On one of those visits, Uncle Joe showed me pictures of models in a magazine. He told me that those models were famous and that I was just as pretty and could be famous too. As he was helping mum get on TV, he would help me become famous too. Mum had been on the TV a couple of times so I knew he was telling the truth. All I had to do was copy what the ladies in the magazine were doing. He would get a friend around to take pictures, because he would have to help me pose and couldn't take pictures at the same time.

The visits became daily for a while. Uncle Joe showed me a lot of different magazines with women and men doing all sorts of strange things with the man's willy. The ladies had hair on their privates in some pictures and not in others. I thought they were probably young like me if they had no hair.

Uncle Joe started showing me photos of other kids and told me those kids were famous. They were doing the same sort of things as the grownups I had been shown. *Must be normal for kids to do this stuff,* I thought, *if mum's okay with it.*

Mum was happy a bit more often as Joe was giving her money to help out with the bills. We were starting to get more toys, but mostly mum would get lots of new clothes and make-up. She said she had to look her best for TV.

I overheard her on the telephone one evening saying, "Are you kidding? Abbie's worth more than that. If you don't give me more money, I'll send one of the other girls." I felt so special, but I didn't go around to see Uncle Joe for a while. Mum said she was waiting for the right time. A few weeks later I heard her talking downstairs, saying how it was almost the amount she wanted and to keep raising the figure. I didn't know at the time, she had them bidding on me.

❧

"What are you doing? For god's sake. All I asked you to do is wash the dishes, and you can't even do that without breaking something. You really are a clumsy little slut aren't you?" The words flew into my ears and I cringed as I saw her coming down the hallway. This woman, my new mother and the cause of my pain, stood over me as I felt an open hand connect with the back of my head. I stumbled forward from the force behind the blow. She went on, "You think you're clever! You're not, you little shit. All you are is a worthless low-life. You should die and give someone else a chance at life. Why don't you just do that? Or should I do it for you?" She rambled on, poison spewing from her lips. Once again the hand flew against me, but this time it was a hammer blow with fist clenched and I fell. She laughed at my feeble attempts to look strong and get away, my pathetic attempts to show her she couldn't hurt me. But inside I knew better, she hurt me, she hurt me really bad all the time. When she paused for a moment I crawled onto my knees then stood up and ran up to my room. It was my only safe place, unless she followed. Sometimes she did and sometimes she didn't.

"That's it! Run away you little weakling. I'm going to kill you one day. I hope you're ready for that," she bellowed. Her threats chased me up the stairs, and I flew into my room and slammed the door.

I screamed out, "No!" I leaned with my back against the door thinking I was strong enough to stop her coming in if she tried.

I cried and tears began to flow down my face. I rubbed my face and eyes with clenched fists so hard to stop the tears. *I am not going to cry. She can't make me cry anymore. I won't let her.*

Once again, she'd succeeded in killing my spirit. I wanted to be strong, but I felt weak inside and out. All she had ever done was hurt me, and I could do nothing about it.

Alex opened the door and saw me huddled in the corner behind my bed. He knew only too well what went on when daddy was out. He came and sat with me but said nothing. Reassurance was pointless. If he said it would be okay, he would be lying, because we both knew it wouldn't be okay, ever. We sometimes sat together and waited in terror, listening to her beat one of the other kids and waiting for her next bout of anger and hatred aimed at us. Several hours later I heard the door open, not my bedroom door but the front door, and I knew instantly that my dad was back. I vaulted up and ran down the stairs to greet him. He looked at me with a gleaming smile. I grabbed him and hugged him as hard as I could, never wanting to let go. It was the only time I ever felt safe, when I was in his arms.

"Oh hello, you're home. How was work?" Mum said. When she saw him hugging me, she walked our way.

"Fine, thanks. Same old, same old. How was your day?" She ignored the question and walked off. Daddy carried me into the lounge. I sat, cradled in his arms, happy again, but just for the weekend.

On Monday morning mum told me I would have the week off school. I had been good all week and so, as a reward, I would be going to stay with a friend for a while. All the other kids were jealous. I remember Alex crying upstairs saying if dad knew, he'd freak. *Knew what?* I asked myself. I couldn't understand why dad would be so upset that I had time off school. Mum gave Alex a good hiding when she heard that and told him, "It's a secret holiday, and if your father finds out, I'll give you such a lashing you won't sit down for a month."

Mum packed me a night bag and said goodbye. When the doorbell rang, she gave me a lecture, telling me not to let her down. Uncle Joe walked in with a big grin. All the kids ran to the door squealing with delight, and as usual he had a pocket full of boiled sweets.

I had no idea it was Uncle Joe I was going with, but when I did realise it, I was happy to get out of there. It was Monday and I hadn't had a beating all day. I looked forward to playing in Uncle Joe's garden. I jumped in his car eagerly waving goodbye and pleased as punch that I got to have a week off school. I hated school.

When we arrived at his house, he had a friend waiting. He seemed very nice. I knew I had seen him before with mum but not for a long time, and I couldn't remember where.

"Don't worry about him," Uncle Joe said. "He's just taking pictures."

I didn't even have time to unpack. Uncle Joe threw my bag into the hallway and pulled me by the hand into the living room. It looked different this time; there was a big, white fluffy carpet and a sheet had been hung covering the wall and the pictures. The sofa had a dark, royal-blue throw over it with white cushions. *Wow, it looks nice,* I thought. He showed me the magazine again and told me to undress and copy the ladies in certain pictures. I felt shy with the man there and Uncle Joe started getting cross.

"Do it properly, how I've taught you, or I will telephone your mother to get round here and sort you out."

"But. . ." It was all I could think to say. I didn't want to upset Uncle Joe. He was always so nice to me.

He went on, "I've spent a long time training you now, don't show me up." He warned me with a "you dare" look. Even though I was sure what I was doing wasn't right, and I hated it, I couldn't stop or mum would beat me even more. Uncle Joe had handed mum an envelope when he arrived at our house, and she was so happy. So I tried to copy the girls in the magazine. I couldn't risk upsetting mum.

I got undressed and sat on the arm of the sofa, cuddling myself. I was cold, exposed, and scared, but what could I do? Uncle Joe came straight over to me and yanked me to my feet. I was shocked. He was never rough with me before. I took a sharp intake of breath and felt the fear rising up in me, my heart beating hard and my legs felt a bit like jelly. Something was different, I sensed it. He had never handled me like that before and it scared me. He pushed me to the floor telling me to lie down. I could feel myself shaking and shivering. It was cold in the house. My stomach was churning, hurting too and I felt so sick. I started to whimper and I could feel a tear run down the side of my face to my ear.

"Open your legs," Uncle Joe said. He didn't wait for me to comply but slapped my legs so hard the stinging made me cry out with pain. He placed his large hand over my mouth and asked if I wanted more. I shook my head no, pleading with eyes wide, tears running freely now.

He took his hand away from my face and eased it slowly down my chest to my tummy he told me, "You only have to do what's in the pictures." His voice calmed, "It's not a big deal." He opened my legs, pulling them wide apart, "Bend your knees and put your feet on the floor," he growled, his eyes piercing me with a stare while exposing my private bits. He put his fingers on my privates spreading them apart, moving aside so the camera got a good shot. Investigating my bits and pulling them around while his friend took pictures. I was so embarrassed, I looked away. He put one finger into me gently moving it in and out a little bit at a time. "Your dry," he said and coughed up some phlegm in his throat and spat at my bits, rubbing harder and faster.

"It burns," I cried. He slapped my legs again, this time with the belt he had taken off and laid beside me.

"Do you want more?" he threatened. My sobs were ignored as Uncle Joe started kissing my private bits. His tongue was warm as he licked me everywhere. His fingers twisted my boobies. He hurt me and it felt like he would pull them off as he bit my nipples.

The man who was taking pictures was getting cross with Uncle Joe, shouting at him, "I have driven hours and paid a fortune to see this shit. So, get on with it and shut her up too."

Uncle Joe unzipped his trousers and, for the first time, took his willy out of his pants and held it to my face.

"Suck it," he said.

"Like a straw?" I asked. He nodded grabbing my hair and twisting it tight between his fingers. "Ouch that hurts!" I cried.

"Lick it," he ordered, pulling my head right up to him. I could hear his breathing getting fast. He seemed in a rush. His willy looked huge. I had never seen a real, full grown one, only the ones in the magazines. I had seen Alex and Daniel when they had a bath, but they didn't look like this, all hairy and purple. It was throbbing against my lips.

I closed my eyes and started to cry when he backed off and smacked me hard across the face. "Now, pull yourself together!" he shouted. "I have full permission from your mum to beat the hell out of you if needed."

I believed him. I took it in my hands and sucked and licked his willy and played with it for what seemed like ages. The man took lots of pictures. Then Uncle Joe rubbed my private parts with his willy until the sticky goo came out, all over me. When he rubbed it on my tummy, I finally realised where the warm cream had come from.

"You're a good girl," he said putting his pants back in place. Your mummy will be very pleased this time."

I felt all icky but I didn't dare ask for a towel.

Uncle Joe looked at the man and said, "That's your lot. Anymore costs a damn sight more." The man handed Uncle Joe a pile of money and walked out the door.

How could he let Uncle Joe do this to me? I thought. *Couldn't he see me crying? He never said a word, just took lots of photos and left. Maybe he'll show someone else what Uncle Joe did.*

Uncle Joe led me by the hand to a bedroom and told me to rest there. I lay on the fresh smelling bed whimpering and wondering what was going to happen. Uncle Joe's telephone kept ringing and I could hear him talking.

"The merchandise is here, prepared and ready," he said several times on different phone calls. I could smell pipe tobacco and it took me back to when my real mummy was alive. For a while I forgot where I was.

I must have drifted into a sleep because when I woke up, it was dark and I could hear voices downstairs. It took a few seconds to register where I was. A car engine started outside bringing me back to reality, and the voices moved from outside to inside the hall downstairs. After a few minutes I heard footsteps coming up the stairs and Uncle Joe opened the door. "Wakey, wakey sleepy head. You've got work to do."

"Work?" I repeated, confused and dazed from sleep and rubbing my eyes.

"Oh yes, honey, you've got to make Uncle Joe some of his money back."

I didn't have a clue what he was talking about. *How do I owe him money?* He led me downstairs with a reassuring arm around my waist.

"Swallow this," he gave me a tablet and a glass of water. "It will make you feel nice."

"No thank you," I said. "I hate tablets."

"I'm not asking, I'm telling," he demanded. "Now swallow the bloody thing."

He led me to the waiting car. "It tastes disgusting," I grimaced.

"Hop in sugar," he opened the door. "You'll be back in the morning."

I hesitated and stepped back, at which point he picked me up by the tops of my arms and threw me onto the back seat. He did it so easily, like you would pick up a doll. I must have been so light to him.

"Any nonsense out here my girl and I will knock your block off," he said.

I didn't know where to look or what to do. The car engine revved quietly then purred while Uncle Joe told the driver, "You have until six in the morning to have her back as there are other bookings."

I couldn't even see the driver; it was pitch black. *Where am I going?* I asked myself. *And with whom?* As the car pulled out of the drive I wondered if I was going home, or rather, hoped I was. But then I remembered mum saying I was away for a week.

The car seemed to travel for ages, I remember starting to feel all silly, my body felt tingly and my head felt like it was going round and round like it was going to fall off. I felt sick for a while but then the sickness passed and I felt weird. I had never felt like this before. I couldn't see straight and my fingers and toes were tingly too. My eyelids were getting heavy but I was too afraid to sleep.

"Where are we going?" I asked the driver. No reply. He didn't say a word the whole time until we got to where we were going. When we arrived the man got out and opened my door and said, "Follow me." There were a few cars where we had parked, all different types. I saw a big white van with an angel and leaves on the side. I remembered the angel because daddy always said I was his angel.

I could tell there were no houses around because all I could see were the shadows of trees, no lights anywhere. We walked and walked through the darkness. The man led me through the night for about 30 minutes to what looked like a barn. I thought we had arrived, but we walked by the barn and carried on walking. I couldn't see very well but there was no one or nothing around. My skin was crawling with nerves, I was cold and shaking and felt sick. I don't know why. Maybe shock from earlier that evening or that silly pill Uncle Joe gave me. We walked a while longer. I could feel long grass scratching my legs and rocks under my feet making it difficult to walk straight without my ankles giving way. I nearly fell over a few times.

The man pushed me on, "Quicker," he said each time I dawdled, shoving me in the back when I started to slow. It was dark and scary like a bad dream. I felt strange, my stomach was in knots with pains shooting in all directions and I was very dizzy. I couldn't walk quickly because the ground was spinning and moving up to meet me. Suddenly, everything went black.

Chapter 6

I could see a light off in the darkness when my eyes opened. *I must have fainted.* The light seemed warm in the night sky, and it seemed to glow for quite a distance. There was nothing else at all that I could see in the pitch black but the light seemed welcoming.

We had been walking for quite a while, the man carrying me in his arms. He was a big man. *His hands are huge,* I thought. I could see him now as I looked up into his face. He was quite tall too. I was never this high up when daddy lifted me. He had short hair and it was very fair. His eyes looked black in the dark and his eyebrows were thick and bushy almost like my daddy's, but daddy's eyebrows met in the middle. His skin was rough, his hands scraping my leg. He put me down when he saw I was awake. He smelt of oil, I knew that smell because I had smelt it before when I went to work with daddy at the truck yard.

The grass was wet and I could feel the wetness seeping through my pumps. The sound of leaves crackling underfoot, twigs that were old and decaying were breaking into a thousand pieces. The rustling broke the silence that surrounded us walking through the woodland. The call of an owl pricked the night and gave life to it. I was still shaking, scared wasn't the word for it. I was petrified!

Tears had dried on my face making it feel tight, and I had a funny taste in my mouth from the silly pill. We reached the bright light at last and the man told me "We're here now." He took my hand in his and guided me up some steps into the house. It looked derelict with no furniture only a fire lit in the middle of the room. The flames lit the room with flickering shadows. Strange drawings hung around the place with all different shapes painted, like stuff we had learnt at school when we were taught about the Egyptians. We walked down a narrow hallway, following the murmurs and sounds of voices. I could hear every footstep because there was no carpet on the floor. I couldn't see anything, it was so dark.

A woman's voice whispered, and for a moment I felt safe, until she said, "I have the camera. Get on with it, time is ticking, time is money, come on!"

Camera? I thought. *I know what that means.*

The man pushed me towards a different man, much older and grey haired into a room off the corridor. He then turned and walked away standing by the door. Almost straight away the old man threw me to the floor in front of him kicking me hard in my stomach. *Why is he kicking me?* I was confused and it felt like my insides were going to split. I screamed but nothing came out apart from a groan. I couldn't breathe. Gasping for breath and clutching my stomach, I curled up my knees to try and ease the pain. There was no carpet, it was just wooden floorboards. They had been painted long ago as it was beginning to peel, leaving thick, rough edges to scratch my skin as I tried to crawl away.

"That's a taster of what's to come if you don't do as you're told," he said.

I looked up and saw there were several people there, men and women. All stood around the outside of the room, saying nothing, just looking at me like I was a zebra in a zoo. Everyone was naked apart from the man who bought me there. I could hear footsteps and a woman walked in. She had three children with her, they looked about seven or eight years old, all girls.

Lots of candles lit the room and the smell of burning wax filled the air. Again I was stripped of clothes for the second time that night. The woman kept clicking photos while the man fiddled with my nipples and pulled my bits around, stretching and pulling, pushing his fingers inside me. I knew I was tearing. I still felt funny after that silly tablet. Every now and then I would feel sick, but I almost felt like it wasn't my body. Sometimes I could feel things and other times I couldn't. A wave of numbness came over me, I couldn't move, my legs wouldn't listen.

The flashing of cameras blinded me. I could see dots dancing in front of my eyes from the bright lights and the flashes stopped me from seeing the other people watching from behind the cameras. *Who are they?* I wondered. *And why won't they help me?*

"Help me!" I screamed, but nobody moved.

A naked woman came over, put her hand on my shoulder and gave me a weird look. A man took pictures while the woman put her head between my legs and licked my bits. She squirted a tube on my bum then pushed a finger inside. Her fingernails were scratchy, but it was as if I had left my body and couldn't feel pain anymore. Her fingers messed around with my privates, one finger in my bum and one finger in my bits, pushing back and forth. On her knees, with her other hand she started to play with her own private parts and moaned and groaned like she was dying. Whilst she did that, her breathing became heavy, and she kept repeating, "Oh my god! Oh my god!" like she was in pain. Her face twisted and creased up as she cried out, "I'm. . . I'm cumming!" *Coming where?* I thought.

She looked like a pretty lady with long black hair almost down to her waist. Her eyes were dark brown and she had really long eyelashes. She wore a long, jewelled necklace that almost reached her stomach. I think she was about mum's age, maybe about thirty years old.

I had mentally gone to another place, a mixture of drugs and indignity. I could feel the fear disappearing. *What am I to do, a nine-year-old girl against a room full of adults?* I couldn't do anything about it. Nothing really mattered anymore, not even when the woman took the camera and told the man, "Now get on with it, there isn't much time left. She is very expensive."

The pain was unbelievable when he rammed his fingers inside me, I could feel the tearing again and there was a warm feeling running down my bottom. I didn't know at the time I was bleeding. He seemed to get really wild as his breathing was heavy and he was banging his knuckles on my bits with his fingers inside.

I couldn't scream; no noise would come out and no one came to my screams anyway. I left this painful world again. I don't know where I went, but I know I stopped feeling pain. It didn't hurt at all when he rammed his willy into my bits. I remember him banging and pushing his body hard onto me, thrusting in and out. I couldn't breathe, he was so heavy but it was like it wasn't my body, I didn't really care. I had given my body up almost like it wasn't mine anymore.

I have no concept how long I was there in that spooky house. Drifting in and out of consciousness, I lost all track of time. The other kids were going through the same as me. In my fog I could hear screams and sobs every now and then, a girl's voice begging, pleading not to hurt her anymore. She spoke with a southern accent too, Cockney I think? Her screams made me shiver so I went to my safe place and stayed there.

When I woke I was being carried into another room. There was a little girl tied down with her legs open. She looked asleep. A man was painting on her with red paint. Another girl was sat on a naked woman's tummy while the woman lay on the floor. The woman was told to suck the girl's boobs. A man licked the woman's private parts and another man squirted his willy all over her. I could see tears running down the girl's face, and when she looked at me and a hand smacked her around the head.

"Concentrate!" she was commanded.

"Smile for the camera," another man said.

For a split second I made eye contact with another girl. She had short, dark hair and bright blue, sad eyes. A tiny scar was on her chin right by her mouth. She was sitting on a pillow posing like a model with a fake smile.

Then I was taken out of the house and carried back to the car. My legs still wouldn't move, they were like jelly. I couldn't walk so I was yanked along half running, half being dragged. I must have fallen asleep again because when I woke up, I was pulled out of the car and carried back into Uncle Joe's house. Uncle Joe gave me a bath and put me to bed, telling me how good I'd been and how it would be easy now. "The first time is always the worst," he said.

When I got out of the bath, he forced me to drink some foul tasting drink, Brandy he called it. He said I would feel better and it would make me sleep. I did sleep, so heavily that when I awoke it was late the next day. My whole body ached. I wanted to cry it hurt so much to move or walk. I found my way to the bathroom and cried quietly while I peed, the burning and stinging sensation on my bits was unbearable.

"You have a day off today," said Uncle Joe with a smile. Not a lot of words passed between us. He offered me different meals of nice food but I wasn't hungry. I watched TV until after the news and was told to get back to bed. "You need your rest," he said.

I was pleased and surprised when Molly knocked at the door the next day. I wanted to tell her what happened, but I had been warned to tell no one. Molly had not been to see Uncle Joe for ages and was really excited because he said she was special. A different friend of Uncle Joe's arrived shortly after, and I knew when I saw the camera it would be more of the same stuff. I felt sick. *Poor Molly,* I thought, *if she only knew.*

Molly refused to take her clothes off, then Uncle Joe changed. He wasn't the nice Uncle Joe anymore. Molly was still crying when he came into the room with a belt. He hit Molly over and over again. She was no stranger to beatings, but Uncle Joe had always been so nice before. He told her there was more of that if she didn't behave herself. He made her take one of the silly pills and then made me take one too. I hated those pills; they made me feel so sick and tasted disgusting. Molly took her clothes off like he said.

For what seemed like hours we were there while the man and Uncle Joe took pictures of us, pictures of me and Molly together, doing poses like the models in the magazines. He told us we had to lick each other's bodies. They took pictures of us licking each other's privates and kissing boobies. Uncle Joe would bend us around until had the pose he wanted. I was sure Molly was just as embarrassed as me, but we had no choice.

Another man came into the house and was watching and playing with his willy while Molly and me did as we were told. We performed for them all. After a while the man handed Uncle Joe a pile of money and took Molly into another room. I could hear her scream for a while then it went quiet. Molly was sent home with an envelope and told she was a very special girl. I had to stay with Uncle Joe for another five days.

I met a lot of his friends. One man came with a big camera and filmed me, like a real life movie star doing grownup games, with different men and ladies. They even brought other kids to be filmed with me, older boys would be told to do different things to me, like push a coke bottle inside me and put a willy in my bum at the same time. I never realised that grownup games hurt so much. Maybe that's why when daddy was home I heard mum groaning and crying out a lot. I started to like the silly pills and ask for them because they took most of the pain away.

I don't think I said much all week. I was like a zombie. I had lost my mind on the pills. It had gone out away from Uncle Joe's house, somewhere it didn't hurt. I pictured myself riding that horse through the fields. It was the only good time that came to mind.

On return to school I was still pretty much in my safe place, in and out of daydreams. I don't remember much of what happened in my class until I had forgotten to give my teacher a letter excusing me from swimming. Mum giving me a letter but I wanted to swim so I forgot on purpose. I couldn't find my own costume so I had no choice but to put on a spare swimsuit.

I don't know why my teacher looked so shocked when I came out of the changing room. There were a few gasps from children in my class, but when I followed their eyes and looked down, there was a trickle of blood running down my legs to the tiles around the pool. Mixed in with water it flew around the outside of the pool filling the grouting between the tiles. My thighs were black and blue with bruises. The teacher ran up, picked me up and wrapped a towel around me. She whisked me up into her arms running to the school office shouting at one of the kids to get another teacher to watch the swimming class.

My class teacher came out of the canteen at the right time to see the swimming teacher carrying me and shouting, "Get help!"

The school nurse asked, "How did you get all those bruises? They're all over your body."   "I don't know," I whispered, blushing and feeling myself disappearing into my safe place.

No way could I talk about it. Remembering things hurt too much. If mum knew I had told she would give me another beating, and I couldn't take any more. I kept my mouth shut and looked away. Part of all the fuss felt good though. It was great to have some 'nice' attention for a change. It felt good to be made a fuss of at school that day. *Does someone really care about me?* I wondered.

After lying down in the nurse's room, I don't know how long I was there. I think I went to sleep, I felt so weak.

My teacher said, "I am so sorry. I'm so sorry sweetheart, I have let you down." Looking around at the clean, white walls which were decorated by pictures of kids at the school, I thought, *They must've drawn them for the nurse.* The glass cupboard had bandages and sticking plasters in one tray, a thermometer sat beside it in another tray and there was a kidney dish beside the bed.

"Just in case you need to be sick," The nurse said, gently rubbing my arm.

Inside the nurse's room, I could hear the head teacher on the telephone. Her office must have been next door to the room I was in. I guessed she was talking to mum, telling whoever, "We are very concerned about Abbie's health. Something must be done and soon, or we will intervene."

I shivered at the thought of what mum would do when I got home.

Chapter 7

St. Catherine's Primary school was not far from our house. It took only about twenty minutes and we would walk to school by ourselves. Mum never took us like a lot of the other mums.

The school was small, typical of schools in the 70's made out of red brick. It had large, glass windows and a flat roof. There were a couple of mobile classrooms in the playground beside a big, plastic, pink elephant slide. Only the little kids were allowed on that. There were at least 200 children in the school and about 30 were in class with Molly and me. We had been in the same classroom together since I started there. I'm glad we were too, because Molly needed me to protect her from the bullying. Molly would never hit back when kids started on her, she was always far too nice.

Things had quietened down at home since the school rang mum. For the last week she hadn't hit me once. In fact she acted like I wasn't even there. She totally ignored me and Alex, almost throwing our plates of dinner on the table and walking away. She seemed to be saying she didn't want us there but found some restraint and never more touched us or even shouted at us.

I was glad the school rang mum. *I wish I had told my teacher sooner,* I thought, *but if I had spilled the beans, would they have believed me?* Hitting kids was pretty normal in those days, even teachers did it. Everyone minded their own business too. My teacher had to know something was wrong, our legs and faces were constantly black and blue. *How could she miss it?* But still neither she nor any of the others did anything to help, all that time. *Our tears must have been invisible,* I thought. *It's the only explanation, invisible tears.* The beatings stopped but not the other stuff. We visited Uncle Joe on and off for the next two years.

On the last day of term before the Christmas break, just as the school bell went, they all ran outside squealing. Everyone was excited after handing out Christmas cards and presents at school. Our class had been making cards for our family, and we had also made a chocolate Yule log in cookery. The thought of Christmas around the corner should have been something to look forward to, but not for me. I never did look forward to holidays; it just gave mum more time to hate us. I didn't like the lessons much but school was my safe haven.

As I neared the gate running with Molly to meet the others, I couldn't believe it when dad walked around the corner. I ran up to him shocked and surprised. No one had ever collected us from school before.

"Dad, dad!" I squealed throwing my arms around his waist. "This is a nice surprise."

"Hello," he said. "Molly, you go on home now with the chocolate Christmas log. I need to speak to Abbie and Alex."

I could see she was upset dad wasn't giving her a lift home too.

It was one week until Christmas and I was eleven years old when dad picked us up from school. It was another big moment when my life would change.

"We're not going home," he said

"Why not?" Alex asked.

We were in the van on the motorway when dad said, "Mum is not a nice person. I'm not taking you back there anymore."

Not a nice person? I thought. *I wonder why it took him so long to find out?*

"Where are we going then?" I asked.

"We're going to see nanny in London for awhile until we get a new house. I've met a nice new lady who is coming to stay with us in London."

My mind was in a whirl. *What about Molly and the others? What about the chocolate Yule log I made? Molly will get to eat it all. That's not fair!*

"Will Santa know where we are?" I asked.

"Yes," he said.

"When will we see our sisters and Daniel again?"

He didn't answer, just ignored me and started driving.

I looked back into the van and saw all of our clothes and a few toys and knew daddy was serious. We drove through the night as I continued to run things through in my mind. I watched the orange street lights go by and wondered what would happen to us.

❦

I hadn't seen my nan or the rest of my family in London for years. When Aunty Helen had visited us last summer, I remembered a huge row she had with mum about bruises on me and Alex. She was ordered out of the house and not to come back. She never did. I wondered, *If she knew what was going on, why not? Why hadn't she told dad? Maybe she did and he wasn't to be bothered!* All I understood was even teachers knew stuff was happening to some degree and did nothing. So, I figured, all that went on must be normal then? This must happen everywhere, maybe that's why all those people had done nothing. There was never a time when I wasn't carrying bruises from something. I had numerous visits to hospital, had my wounds stitched and bruises tended too, but not one person ever lifted a finger. *Was it normal for a child to have belt buckle marks across their back?* I wondered.

When I awoke we were still travelling. I lay in the van staring through the side window, amazed at the buildings and the street lights of London. I didn't remember going to London for years but I was aware I lived there as a baby. My dad came from a typical Irish family with eight brothers and one sister. They all had children of their own as good Catholic families do. Dad said a lot of relations wanted to meet us, apparently over the next few days, Aunts, Uncles and plenty of cousins. It would be exciting to meet them, but for now I wondered what would happen to Molly. Who was to protect her when I was gone? We had a special relationship, so why couldn't dad bring her too?

I must have said it aloud as dad mumbled, "She's not mine, just you and Alex are." With that I felt his warm hand stroke my hair. "It will be all right honey, we'll be fine." I fell asleep again.

The grinding noise of the sliding van door woke me, and very sleepily I looked around, rubbing my eyes all I could see were millions of houses. They all looked the same, all grey concrete and pebble dashed. *Which one is nans? How would I find it if I ever went out alone?* There was a new smell in the air, not a nasty smell but not the clean country air smell I had been used to. Alex stood at the back of the van helping dad unload all the bags. I sat in the van frozen with fear. I didn't know anyone and this place was a foreign as the moon.

A soft Irish accent called my name from outside the van, "Abbie? Where is she?" the voice asked dad and at the same time a head popped around the corner smiling at me. "Come on chicken," she said smiling and offering me her hand.

I couldn't remember nan at all, but I could remember her voice and that Irish accent I found so soothing, but amusing too. She took me into the kitchen and made some Horlicks for Alex and me. I remembered the last time we had Horlicks was when we went to live with someone else after our mummy died. She sliced some fresh bread on a wooden chopping board in the middle of the kitchen table. The table was covered in brightly coloured plastic table cloth and had different types of sauce bottles in the middle. She buttered it with real butter out of the butter dish and I stood in shock and watched as she sprinkled sugar all over it. I had never tasted anything so good. The sugar made my mouth come alive, the bread was so soft and fresh and I don't think it touched the sides.

"Och be Jesus! This girl needs feeding up," she yelled at dad as he walked in the door with yet more black bags. "She must be half the weight she should be, poor wee cow."

Dad grunted and mumbled something to nan, at which point, to my horror and utter surprise she stood up. Being a lot smaller than dad, it was even more shocking to see the way she dived at him slapping him fast and hard around the face.

"What have you let her do to these kids?" she yelled.

Holy Mary, mother of God! I almost fell off my chair.

She ran on, "Their mother would be turning in her grave poor cow, and look at her legs aw-be-Jesus, look at her Paddy!" She must have seen my legs when I was sitting on the floor. She pulled me close yanking my skirt down to the floor and exposing my pasty, thin legs. They were covered in long thin cane marks. Purple, yellow and green bruises covered most of my thighs. She lifted my top and turned me so my dad got a good look at my back. She looked at dad then pulled my top down, stroked my face gently and walked away shaking her head and muttering under her breath.

I looked at daddy and saw shame written all over his face. I had never seen him look at me quite that way before. He almost looked mad at me. He looked upset and in pain. *Is that because nan hit him?* I wondered. *Or because of seeing my bruises? I don't know.* Maybe he felt embarrassed like a child again in front of his mum getting told off? Finally, he smiled and rubbed my head before walking out of room and lighting a cigarette.

I awoke the next morning smelling bacon being cooked--to this day I love that smell. Cooked breakfast with mum had not only been rare but even when she cooked breakfast for dad at weekends, we never used to get any, only left-overs. Nan called me to the kitchen. The radio was playing quietly and the room was filled with the smells of cooking bacon and sausages. Nan stood by the cooker frying bread and nodding towards the table.

"Abbie, get seated and start your eating," she smiled pointing towards a chair. I took a slice of bacon and a sausage and started to eat. I wasn't really hungry.

To be honest, my mind was still whirling thinking how Molly would love this food. She always did have an appetite even when I would refuse to eat what mum had dished up, things like tripe or sheep's brains, kidneys or liver. My mind raced back to mum trying to force fish into my mouth the day before. The fish bits and guts were a favourite of hers. She got a good deal from the guy at the market, saying they were for our cat but really they were for us kids. It was disgusting, there were eyes and bits of skin and bones, but mum thought it was good for us. She would try and make it edible by frying onions with it. The day before she had held my nose and forced me to choke it down. I had pretended to eat some but went straight to the toilet and spit it out down the loo. I did that quite a lot. I was mad at myself for thinking about mum, *Why can't I get her out of my mind?*

"Don't you like it?" nan said scanning my plate. "What a face. You look like I'm trying to poison you."

"I do like it, but I'm not very hungry," I replied quietly. I was expecting a slap or something for not eating and answering back.

"Come on honey," she tried to persuade me for at least an hour.

I did my best but I was feeling so worried about Molly and the rest of the kids. Alex never had a problem with his appetite. He was tucking into breakfast and looking at me like everything was normal. His blue eyes sparkled as he smiled and his scruffy, curly morning hair all over the place. I returned a smile, but it came from my mouth and not my heart.

I could smell he had been wet and wondered if nan would be angry. He was eleven years old now and mum would say, he shouldn't be wetting the bed. She would even send him out to play with a nappy on for punishment. I hoped nan wouldn't smell it too; that would spoil how nice she was being. As the morning went on nan was busy doing the housework and let us do whatever we wanted.

"Your bath is ready," nan called to where I was watching TV.

I had never seen Saturday morning TV. If we were at home with mum we had to go out to play. I walked through to the bathroom and waited for nan to leave before slipping into the water. Nan knocked on the door after a while to check on me and came in to find me under water, seeing how long I could hold my breath. I had never been able to win before. Molly would always hold her breath longer than me.

Nan coming in made me jump up fast. At home we didn't have baths very often and when we did, it was for a scrubbing down. *Did nan come in to scrub me down?*

Seeing how embarrassed I was, she walked out and pulled the door too. "Your Aunty Helen is coming to visit today," she called through a gap in the door.

I hadn't seen Aunty Helen since mum chucked her out of the house.

Chapter 8

The following morning I awoke to hear voices talking in the kitchen. It took a few seconds to remember where I was. Nan's house was a council house, pebble-dashed outside, a terraced house in what looked like a jungle of terraced houses. They all looked exactly the same apart from individual curtains and plants in the gardens. I was staying in the spare room with Alex; he slept on the floor on a mattress. The wallpaper had big pink roses all over it and they looked so real, almost like you could reach over and pick one up. The curtains were white with pink stripes and the carpet was red with orange and white patterns. It looked old and worn by the door. Nan had lots of different ornaments on the fireplace, all different green Leprechauns on one side and glass cats on the other. In the middle of the shelf was a large glass vase; in the bottom of it was a small brown China mouse. Clinging onto the side about to climb in the vase was a grey China cat. *Poor mouse,* I thought.

Whilst I was getting dressed in the clothes nan had put out for me, I could hear the voices were getting louder and angrier.

"I'd of had 'em!" Aunty Helen shouted in her Cockney accent. "Why on earth leave em there when you knew what she was doing? You worked away all week, every week and left her to do what she liked to your kids." There was silence, I didn't know who this was aimed at, but I guessed it was probably dad. I felt sorry for him. He had never done anything wrong to me as far as I knew, but everyone was treating him like he was the one who beat me up.

"I never saw you go running back there to try and help those kids after she kicked you out," dad bit back. "You're just as much to blame."

I heard a lot of talk that I really wasn't meant to hear, either through open doors or pretending to be asleep when I wasn't. I found out that all my uncles had known what mum was doing to us when dad had gone. Even our neighbours had complained to dad and even rang the police when mum had gone out with one of her boyfriends and locked us in the house for the night. No doubt they must have heard us kids screaming when we were getting a beating or having our heads banged off the wall to "knock some sense into us." No one ever mentioned Uncle Joe though, so I guessed they didn't know that bit.

They spoke about how mum's own kids got all the nice new clothes and toys whilst Alex and I got clothes from charity. It reminded me of an occasion at school when one of my friends accused me of stealing her coat. It turned out she had seen her name in the collar and her mum hadn't told her she had given it to the charity shop. That friend then told everyone at school how I had stolen her coat and that I wore tramp's clothes.

I overheard one of my uncles saying that no one from this side of the family knew for quite a while that my real mum had died. When I heard that I thought to myself, *What could they have done even if they had known?* No one could have been aware that our new mum got her kicks from picking on kids.

As I sat listening to the grownups in the other room my mind drifted away thinking of how me and Alex were treated differently. All the things I was overhearing made me realise the things that had been happening to me were not normal.

It didn't take long--once something triggered it off--for me to be back into my world of hatred, my world of pain. Every day my mind slipped back to when my stepmother tortured us and tried to kill my spirit. I started feeling bad all the time. Every moment I was there, my anger built up inside me, and my life fell back to an all-time low. My thoughts and hopes and dreams were soon smashed out of me, as once again violence struck. I knew that the anger against my stepmother had built to a point of no return. My mind wandered back into dark memories. Fists came at me from nowhere, blood dripping from my nose and ear. Mum walked patiently around me, waiting for me to break and cry. It was her game, her way of controlling me and making me suffer. She stopped only when I could fight no more.

I shook my head but all I could think about were those dark memories. I remembered coming home from school once and being dragged to the bathroom. The look in her eye was crazed, her eyes glazed over when she was in one of those moods. I had learnt to stay away from her, but sometimes she planned things and on that particular day she had known exactly what she was doing.

"You are disgusting," she screamed in my face slapping me around the head. My facial skin felt like it was burning off. I had that giddy feeling that you only get as a kid.

"I've had a letter from school," she said throwing it at me. "You've got head lice, you dirty slut!" With that I was picked up and thrown into the bath. It was full of freezing cold water smelling of bleach.

"I'll get you clean once and for all," she yelled. She scrubbed me from head to foot with the floor scrubbing brush. My eyes were stinging, my skin was burning, but all I could do was sit there and take it. Inside my head was screaming and wishing I could have a silly pill. But the tears didn't come out as I struggled to get away slipping in the bath, feeling like a rag doll, a lifeless body getting flung around. As my head was pushed under I wished I could remain under water forever and never come up. But Molly and I had been practising how long we could stay under water so I survived the dunkings.

"What's wrong with you?" mum screamed continuing to shake me. "How dare you embarrass me like that? In future wash properly then this won't happen will it?"

"I will, I promise," I said, rubbing my stinging eyes. I was hauled out of the bath. My eyes were in agony and I couldn't see properly. All I could hear were scissors clipping and cutting away at my lovely, golden brown hair. Everyone used to comment on how nice my hair looked. But now, my hair was shorter than my brother's and I felt like a boy. I felt ugly and dirty and was sent to bed with no dinner.

Mum had been forced to take me to see the doctor after my skin and eyes reacted to the bleach. He gave me eye-drops and cream for my skin. Mum told him I had thought the bleach was bubble bath after she had changed brands. The Doctor believed her, again.

The voices were getting louder, bringing me back to my senses, "Stay here for a while!" nan pleaded. "They've been through enough don't cha know?"

Dad said he had to go to work in the morning so we would stay with nan while things got sorted.

Nan was a hard lady to say "no" to. No one argued with her, not even grand-dad. Nan smelt of lavender, and her hands used to shake for no reason. "Parkinson's," my aunt called it.

Maggie was arriving in a few days, I heard them say.

"Maggie? Who's Maggie?" I asked Alex.

"I think it's dad's new girlfriend," he shrugged.

"New girlfriend?" I walked into the warm kitchen and asked Nan.

"Yes," she spat back.

I could tell she wasn't very impressed about this Maggie person. Nan said we needed "TLC" and lots of it, never mind competing with more kids. Maggie had three kids of her own but they wouldn't be coming straight away.

"Great, more kids to share dad with!" Alex snapped back sarcastically.

I hadn't thought of it that way, but there was no way I was sharing MY dad again. I agreed with Alex.

Little did I know that everything had already been arranged and Maggie was on her way to be with us permanently.

My aunty had arranged for me to go to school in London. I hated it! Being the new girl, everybody stared at me. They would look at me a giggle.

"I look like a boy, I know I do," I complained to nan when she asked how my day had gone.

"I hate school. I don't want to go there again. The teachers don't do anything and everyone is picking on me," I moaned at nan for hours that night.

The next morning nan instructed my aunty to escort me to school demanding to see the head of year. She disappeared into an office and re-appeared again after about 20 minutes, apologising to the head teacher for wasting her time. She grabbed my arm and told me lying is not going to stop me from going to school, so I had better just get on with it. She told me if anyone started on me to, "Sort them out big time!" I thought that meant to smack them one. So that's what I did the very next day. That was how it always got sorted in London.

My aunt was called into school again, this time it was because I had hit several pupils. I was not very patient with anybody and when I hit someone "usually for no real reason," I felt so good for ages afterwards. It had a real calming effect like I had been given that sugar sandwich all over again. The kids at that school didn't bother me much after that. If they did annoy me, they soon learnt not to. Boys or girls it didn't matter. No one scared me because I had no fear. What on earth could they do compared to what my mum had done? *If they only knew what I survived, they would leave me alone,* I thought, but I never mentioned anything to anyone.

I did start to make friends, but I think it was more because the kids thought it was better to be my friend than my enemy. Kids left Alex alone too. My reputation for trouble had spread to years above me.

"Get ready," Nan shouted from the kitchen through to the garden, "Your dad is arriving with his new girlfriend." Alex and I looked at each other not saying anything, but with knowing thoughts. We headed inside to meet the infamous Maggie.

Chapter 9

She sat in the front of dad's Volkswagen camper van. He loved that car and was always tinkering with this or that on it. Dad was so proud he was constantly washing it, usually with Alex in tow. It was orange and white outside with orange stretchy seats inside, the curtains where brown and cream.

Disgusting, I thought.

It looked like she was scared to get out and she was arguing with dad, her hands waving around frantically. As we peered out the window, it seemed she was pleading with him. Dad was obviously trying to calm her down. She looked over toward me and saw me looking from behind the curtain. I wish I could have smiled to make her feel more at ease, but the truth was, I didn't want to smile. I wanted her to go back to where she came from. *Who is this woman?* I wondered. *What is so special that dad would leave mum? And what about her kids? What about Molly, Debbie, Daniel and Kassie? This Maggie must be something!*

She had shoulder length, dark brown, permed hair and pale blue eyes that sparkled with life. She spoke with a soft Welsh accent and she was slim but not skinny. *Her boobs aren't as big as mum's,* I noticed. "A good figure," I heard nan say to

Aunty Helen. She was very pretty. Her face had fine features, and I could see why dad liked her but she did seem quite shy. I was happy for that; maybe she would leave me alone.

I didn't want to be friends with her.

Dad asked of me before he left for work, "All I want is for you to get on and be friends."

Who is he kidding? I thought to myself. *Keep me out of it. You want her, not me. You be nice.*

Once inside I heard her talking with nan.

"If you love him, you will leave your kids in Scotland!" Nan screamed at Maggie.

"But they are my kids. I love them. How could I possibly leave them?" Maggie cried. I could hear her sobbing.

I expect nan was just trying to protect us, but I did feel a bit sorry for Maggie. Nan was not a person one disagreed with.

I heard Maggie on the phone with dad that night. "Get me out of here right now!" she shouted down the telephone at him, "I will not stay here one day longer, do you hear me?"

I thought whilst lying in my bed that night that Maggie deserved everything she got. Serves her right for splitting up me and my sisters. I was getting to quite like my bed. It was so warm with the blankets and patchwork quilt on top. Nan said she made it herself so it meant even more to me. I lay there thinking, if nan didn't like Maggie, then there must be a reason. Nan was the only person on the planet I trusted. She had been the only one who understood my plight, so I would stay loyal to her no matter what.

❧

We climbed the stairs to the flat we were looking at. It was massive. The block had only four flats with a shared garden space. Waltzing through the rooms Maggie was excited saying how Alex would have his own bedroom. I would have my own bedroom too, and her own boys would share, because they were brothers.

My room was small and a funny shape. It had alcoves all around. Dad said it should have been a library; the window was arched and opened with a lot of huffing and puffing. It was old and a bit stuck where someone had painted on the runners. "We'll fix that," he reassured me. But I didn't mind. It was the first time since mum died I had ever thought of having my own room. It looked out over the garden. I wondered who lived in the other flats, *Do they have kids? Will they be nice?*

"It's not perfect but it will do for now," Maggie said. Dad didn't look at all impressed.

Maggie put her hands on her hips and said, "I will not spend another night at your mother's house."

"Now Maggie," dad said.

"We've been there a week, and that's six days too long in my book. So it's this flat, right now, or I leave! The choice is yours, Sean."

"That's my nan you're talking about," I said under my breath. She didn't hear me.

My attitude was deteriorating rapidly, and I was getting brave. Dad was working away again and only back at weekends. I had started helping myself to Maggie's purse. I had begun smoking and needed cash. If Maggie knew I was stealing from her, she never let on.

It was the start of yet another school for me. This time I went to school with a whole new attitude. It must have been an "If you dare" attitude, because the girls didn't pick on me at all. My hair had grown and I started to bud out a bit, so I was looking more like a girl. I became quite popular at school, helped by the fact that I always had cigarettes and usually plenty of money to spend at dinner time when we went to the shops.

I got on well with Maggie's kids too. They were a bit quieter than I was used to, but they were nice enough. I put it down to the fact they were nervous because they didn't know any of us. Keith was just four years old and so cute. The older two, Gavin and Sean, were similar ages to Alex and me. I didn't have much to do with them though, probably because I was a girl.

I remember when Maggie's kids went to visit their dad for a day and never came back. Maggie was devastated! Her ex-husband told her that if she wanted her kids they would have to go to court and choose who they wanted to live with. Maggie refused not wanting to put her kids through that. So she left them with their dad. I expect she never stopped loving them though and, in a way, I think she felt resentment that we were there, and not her own kids. But, then again, she did often say how pleased she was she had a daughter at last. One thing is for sure though. I admired the courage it took for her to stand her ground. It must have eaten her up missing her kids and all.

We didn't stay at the flat for long, maybe three months. Dad had been offered another job for more money, so we were to be moving houses yet again. Wiltshire wasn't too far away. I was twelve years old had been to six schools. I wasn't looking forward to moving again. I started the new school and surprisingly, I loved it straight away. I made friends quickly. Proud of myself, I was even getting good at making friends and that included boyfriends.

I soon had a boyfriend named Tom. I never worried when he touched me. He didn't try to do more than put his hand up my top or down my knickers. I found it all pretty boring really, but Tom seemed to get a kick out of it.

What is it about me? I wondered. *I always seem to attract people that want to touch me.* My friend Lucy's dad was no different. He would walk me home and insist on having a kiss. He would fumble around my top, breathing his cigarette breath into my mouth.

"You're beautiful," he would say as he kissed me goodbye each time.

I would run inside and brush my teeth. He was ugly and his teeth were stained and rotten. I could still taste him and the fags hours later despite the fact I smoked. His taste always stayed with me.

I knew Lucy was kissed that way by her dad too. I saw him go into the bathroom with her when I stayed over one night. Her mum had gone to Bingo with her friends leaving him to babysit with Lucy and me. Lucy had gone to the bathroom to get changed. She was in there a while, so I went to see what she was doing as we were supposed to be having a feast in her room. As I approached the bathroom I was about to knock and call her when I heard a whimpering cry, followed by a slap. That perked my ears and I was frozen stiff.

"Just fucking do it," I heard her dad say in a forceful demand.

"Please dad not now, Abbie is here," Lucy pleaded.

I heard another slap followed by, "Suck it. . . good, now lick it or shall I get your friend to do it for you?" I was scared but I couldn't help listening through the door. It went quiet for awhile apart from a few quiet grunts and groans and whispering from her dad. Then I heard him say louder, "I'm telling you for the last time, open your fucking legs or I will walk straight into your bedroom and service your friend. Got it? She's far prettier than you anyway."

I knew what he was doing to her. I could hear his grunts louder and louder and Lucy crying, then all went quiet. I ran to my bed that had been made up on the floor and pretended to be asleep.

Stretching my arms up as if I had just woken up, I said to her, "Oh there you are, I must have nodded off." What could I say? I knew what had just happened. I assumed it was probably best for now that she didn't know I knew. I could see she was upset. It happened enough times with Uncle Joe and others for me to know the score.

Lucy's dad started kissing and touching me a few weeks after that night. He told me that if I told anyone, Lucy would be put into a children's home. He said she was only kept there because he liked me to visit. If I stopped pleasing him then he didn't want Lucy anymore. She was my best friend and a bit of kissing and touching didn't bother me really, after all I'd been through. Uncle Joe had fooled around a lot more than that and the way Lucy's dad fiddled with my privates was no different. It didn't seem to bother me that much. *It's what men do after all*, I told myself. *Isn't it?* I didn't know any better.

Chapter 10

Memories of riding horses always haunted me, in a good way though. I never forgot how it felt to ride that stallion when I was nine. I just knew I had to be around them. I would dream of riding horses bareback on beaches or galloping through woods ducking to avoid trees. The feeling of power when that horse surged, and the wind built was something I would never forget. Those dreams kept me going many a boring day at school whilst I stared out of the window.

I was twelve when I started helping at the yard. It was an hour's walk either way, but helping wasn't enough. I wanted to ride more and more, so I began stealing money to pay for riding lessons. There was a big riding school there. They had horses of all sizes from little Shetlands to big Hunters. I loved them all, and it didn't take me long to learn all their names and where they slept.

The stable manager would often ask where the money came from. It was "Birthday money" or "Christmas money," I would say. I wasn't about to tell her it was stolen, money that Maggie had put away in her wardrobe, the savings she had hidden to pay the bills. I got too clever for my own good and stole over £100 in one go. I handed the money over to the riding school saying I wanted to "block book" some lessons. It didn't take Maggie long to figure out who had taken the money.

"That's it!" she screamed. I knew she was upset as she didn't get cross with me very often. "Get in your room and don't come out!" she bellowed pointing the way. I had a nice room and I didn't mind at all. Maggie didn't deserve the trouble I gave her. She had been very upset after her kids had gone to see their dad. I could hear her crying at night, sobbing about her boys and how she loved them and wanted them back. I felt so jealous. *I wish someone loved me that much.* I heard Maggie, on the phone to her ex husband, pleading to let her have her children back. She did what she did out of love for those kids, but I know people looked at her as if she deserted them. I knew different. She loved them so much I hated it, and I hated her for it.

We would go on visits to see them, but you could tell her kids were upset. They thought she didn't want them. Well, that's what her ex told them. He was doing a great job in turning the kids against Maggie. As much as I didn't want another mum--after all, I'd had two already--I hated seeing how much she was hurting. I just wished someone cared that much about me. It didn't take long before her kids stopped wanting to see her.

My mind finished wandering and I was jolted back into the present with her voice screaming at me. She was angry, so angry with me stealing her money.

"You wait until I speak to your father," she said, slamming the door to my room. I didn't mind, I liked my own space. I would sit there for hours listening to music or playing with my tape recorder, the one with the big, round reels of tape? That's what we had back in the 70's. Enid Blyton and my grey, long-haired hamster called Fluff kept me occupied for hours.

Dad never said anything when he returned at the weekend, nothing, that is, until I wanted to go to the stables.

"No way," dad said. It isn't happening again.

My mind went into pieces! I had decided that horses were my life.

"There is no point in living, if it's without horses," I screamed. "What else do I have?"

Dad ignored my pleas and told me to get used to the idea as we soon would be moving house again.

Great! I thought, rambling on inside my brain. *I feel like a Gypsy, nowhere is home. Every time it's the same. As soon as I make friends I have to move and start all over again. What about Lucy? What will happen to her without me there to keep her dad at bay? Will he really put her in a kid's home?*

Knowing that everyone at the stables would know I was a thief was the only thing that stopped me from going there. I didn't know what to do with myself so I started hanging around with my boyfriend, Chris, and his friends. They were into "Rock and Roll" and we would spend many a night going to disco's for Rock-a-Billy's. Chris would spend more time doing his hair than any woman I knew, making sure his quiff was "just so." It was about that time that I began stealing booze and drinking in secret. At twelve years old I had major attitude issues and was far too "grown up" to be told what to do.

As much as Maggie would try to give me boundaries or curfews or tell me off when I had been out of order, nothing worked. *Grounded? Not me.* I was on a downward spiral of self-destruction and I totally ignored her. *Who does she think she is telling me what to do?* I was angry with the world for letting me down and carried it with me like a solid block of concrete on my shoulder. It was evident in everything I did. Dad was never there to back Maggie up. In a way she was like a glorified babysitter, looking after me and Alex while dad was away at work. I guess all of his wives had been babysitters, after all he was always on the road.

When we moved to Kent a few weeks later, I totally shut down, another house move had made something pop in my head. I didn't listen to anyone, and I didn't smile very often. I didn't even know it then but I had put barriers up. Pretty much everyone who had been in my life so far had hurt me. No one could protect me, so I mentally figured I could do a better job myself by shutting everyone out. I totally lost contact with Lucy; I never learned what happened to her.

My new school was situated at the top of a valley and was by far the biggest school I had attended.

"Reading your report from your previous school leaves a lot to be desired," barked the new head teacher. "We will not put up with that kind of behaviour here."

I stood there looking at the floor, thinking to myself, *'Blah fucking blah fucking blah, get on with it!'* Counting how many small wooden tiles were on the floor of his large office, surrounded by bookshelves, I felt sort of intimidated. He looked very official. I could feel my cheeks getting warm as he lectured me about school rules and standards.

Really? I thought. *I bet you just want to do things to me too but haven't got the nerve to say it!*

"Follow me," he said, standing up and marching towards the door. "You can go now," he said to Maggie, dismissing her. She leaned forward to kiss me and I turned my cheek and walked on to follow the head teacher. I didn't even look back. I wanted to so much, but I figured if I didn't like her at all then I wouldn't be hurt if she let me down or if dad buggered off with someone else!

I could feel the eyes burning my back as we marched along long corridors, out into a playground and we headed towards a wooden mobile classroom. I could feel the staring from the kids and I caught hold of a few which I met with an icy glare. I didn't feel like returning the smiles, I just looked away and disappeared into dreamland whilst I was being introduced to the class of other spotty thirteen-year-olds.

The first day of school went grudgingly slow. I found where the kids went that smoked cigarettes and spent all of my breaks there. As the school bell rang to return to class, I was caught by the head teacher.

He said, "By the way young lady, less of the makeup."

Less makeup? Who are you trying to kid? My makeup is part of my way of life.

I discovered being a modette was a brilliant way of hiding my true self. The black "bitch lines" on my eyelids defined me, as did the micro-miniskirts. My hair was dyed jet black and cut into a Mary Quant Bob. I looked like I had been pulled out of a 60's magazine like the thin model, Twiggy, and that was my intention. Out of school I would scour the charity shops seeking the latest bargain in authentic 60's clothing so I could look the part. I had the attitude to match.

It didn't take long before I was playing truant on a regular basis. Maggie kept pleading with me to "be more like Alex" and get on with my studies. "Alex is doing so well at school." He was not far from doing his exams and was, "going to do very well in life." I overheard Maggie telling dad, "Why can't Abbie settle down? It's been months now."

If only they knew, I thought. If only they knew that Alex wasn't this little, blue eyed angel they thought he was. I was still covering for him, still taking the blame when something he had stolen got found out. I was the one who took the blame, who admitted to stealing dad's alcohol or his fags. It was Alex who picked the lock on the telephone and ran up the bills, and me who took the blame. I guess I just looked guilty.

Yes Alex is doing so well! Well, I suppose compared to me he was. I had started to run away for weekends. Maggie wouldn't let me go when I asked; she said I was too young for those parties. *Too young? I'm thirteen damn it!* I certainly felt like an adult and had experienced a lot more that most young adults. *To hell with Maggie!* I decided to go anyway. *How is she or anyone else going to stop me?*

The mod scene totally took over my life. I became even harder to reach. I would steal money on a regular basis, or if no money was available, I would steal something of Maggie's or dad's and pawn it for cash. Part of me hated doing it; the other part stuck a finger up at her and everyone else.

One weekend I had stolen cash from Maggie's purse and hitched a ride to Scarborough. There was a Scooter Rally going on that weekend, and if you were "anyone," you were there. I had no choice I had to go. I would never live it down with my mates if I didn't, so I packed my bag and just up and left. I often ran away to the streets of a big city or a scooter rally and tried to lose myself among the crowds. Other kids like me, kids who were running from one thing or another, all had a history locked inside that no one could reach. The streets were full of them.

The buzz that I got on rallies was electrifying. There were scooters everywhere, literally thousands of them. Mods and scooterists lined the road on both sides, new arrivals driving down the centre like a parade. Police directed scooters where they wanted them to park. It was heaving, the air thick with exhaust fumes and adrenaline. The Best scooters and Coolest mods would ride up and down so everyone could admire their fancy paint jobs, amazing artwork. Some scooters looked like they should be framed in an art gallery.

Everyone would be dressed to kill. They thought they were cool and so did I. I spent hours getting ready. I died my hair black again renewing its glossy shine. This time it was cut in a Quant five point bob, back combed into a beehive at the top. My bitch lines were done to perfection. I could even do them without a mirror and they were perfectly straight. I wore the palest pink, almost white lipstick. I wore a black and white checked mini dress, white calf-length PVC boots and a white matching clutch bag. I had found both boots and bag for £1.00 from Oxfam.

I look good! I thought. Heads were turning, and I knew I could pull tonight. Well I needed to because I had nowhere to sleep. Most would take a tent or book up hotels or bed and breakfasts if they had cash, but a lot of people would just find somewhere that was dry to "crash."

I was approached by a smart looking mod guy, dressed in a two-tone, blue suit, Chelsea boots and Fishtail Parka coat. He looked the part with his button down shirt and thin one-inch tie. But I strutted in my usual "you're not good enough to walk on the same side of the road as me" attitude. I think he liked it. He followed me down the road trying to look cool but working to pull me at the same time. I couldn't make it too easy for him, but eventually gave in and agreed to meet him later at the dance hall. There was to be a dance there tonight, with 60's music and "Northern Soul." I agreed, secretly hoping I had found a bed for the night.

The sweet music pounded out of the doors of the dance hall. *Back Stabbers* by the O'Jays, what a tune! Everyone was having a great time dancing and popping pills to help them feel even better and more relaxed. I had my first "voluntary" pill that night, and the sensation was weird. It seemed so much different than when I had been forced to take those silly pills before. My whole body relaxed but I felt happier than I had been in years. I danced the night away oblivious to my new found stalker who had given me the pills. He wasn't too bad looking if the truth be known and he had a lot of friends with him too. They had driven up from Shepherds Bush in London, my home town. I thought to myself, *Most mods dream of living in the City, where the action is. One day I will be back in London.*

London was the coolest place to be if you were a mod; the clothes shops in Carnaby Street were the best. They had the most original clothes that everyone looked for, but one had to pay the price. It wasn't cheap. The clubs around Shepherds Bush catered to mod music with live bands. It was heaven, I planned to go back soon.

The night passed in a cloudy blur. The dance was so packed I was relieved to be helped and guided outside by my new friend. The fresh air hit me like a sack of spuds. I was drunk, even though I didn't remember drinking that much. It was the pills I guessed. We walked along the beach, as I listened to the sound of waves rushing up onto the sand and smacking off rocks. The waves teased the pebbles going in and through them while they lay lifeless being tossed around with no control. *It's just like me,* I thought. But the sea gave a sense of freedom and power. I sat down in the sand and stared out into the distance. For the first time that I could ever remember, I felt alive, free and relaxed. The salty wind blowing in my face made me come to my senses for a second and I felt my knotty hair.

"How the hell am I gonna get a brush through this after the wind has finished with it?" I threw my head back giggling and lay down on the sand, staring up at the stars. I didn't want the night to end. I could hear giggling farther down the beach and even farther away, behind us, I heard the chorus of a gang of lads singing.

"We are the mods, we are the mods, we are, we are, we are the mods," they sang. *This is the life,* I thought. Being a mod was a way of life, and it was that night I realised it had got hold of my soul.

Gary, my new friend, lay down beside me. He turned on his side looking my way. I still felt good and it only made sense to share it with someone. I knew I would have to perform sexual acts tonight, especially if I wanted a warm bed, so I didn't resist at all when Gary leant over and kissed my neck. He moved straight on top of me and in a bit of a fumble he undid his trousers, pulled off my knickers and slipped his dick inside me.

I hadn't had full sex for a couple of years and it hurt a bit. I felt myself tense, and as Gary was banging away, my mind wandered off, back to Uncle Joe's. Just like I had done there, I went off to my safe place and didn't feel Gary anymore. I felt myself sinking away, like I was going deeper and deeper into a tunnel. It was dark and the deeper I went, the darker and quieter it became. I liked it there.

When I woke up I was alone on the beach. My clothes were a mess; my skirt was up around my waist and my knickers were on the sand. I looked like I had been raped, but I knew I hadn't. *It was definitely consensual, I'm sure of it,* I thought, although my memory was a bit foggy due to the drugs. I really had no worries about my body, even if it had been used and abused. I didn't care. I used my body as a tool to get what I wanted. I had neither pride in it nor fear of it.

The sun was rising and I rushed to my feet in a panic, looking around to see if anyone was nearby that could see me like that. *Pheeew, no one around.* It was silent apart from the waves crashing and the odd seagull waking up, calling and screeching for breakfast.

I made my way up to the road and looked for a public toilet to sort myself out. I remember giggling when I found one. On opening the door to the strong smell of ammonia, I was greeted by bodies everywhere in sleeping bags. People obviously couldn't afford a hotel so they crashed in the loos. I made myself presentable, re-doing my bouffant hair and applying my liquid, black eyeliner to touch up the bitch lines that were crumbling away. After a dab of lipstick I looked in the mirror and thought, *Okay, back in business.*

It was another day, a day to be who I wanted to be and not what anybody else wanted me to be. The day was the same as the one before, lots of posing on scooters, showing off clothes and looking cool, well, attempting to anyway.

I met up with some lads from Hampshire and spent the day with them. They looked smart and I wasn't ashamed to hang with them. I quite liked one of lads, Greg his name was. He had short, fair hair and the most shocking blue eyes. I fancied him straight away and I could tell he knew it. I felt all silly around him. But I knew that after the Bank Holiday weekend was over, I would probably never see him again, so I refused to let myself get carried away. There was no point in him having my number as I was never at home anyway.

During the day, lots of fights broke out with skinheads. I found that fighting gave me an adrenaline rush, something I hadn't felt since riding horses. It didn't take much and I was hooked. I started fights for even looking at me the wrong way. Greg looked out for me grabbing my hand as we ran down the side streets shouting, "We are the mods!" all in chorus. We smashed shop windows and anything in our path. I laughed so much I thought my sides would split. There must have been at least sixty or seventy of us running like a pack of dogs, not giving a toss about anything. We were being ourselves, being free from rules and totally out of control. It felt great. We did our best to out-run the police that had pulled up in vans, lots of them in riot gear. They attempted to block our access to other parts of town, herding us like sheep where they wanted us to go and where we would cause the least amount of damage.

Greg kissed me lightly on my lips later that night, and together we wished the weekend wouldn't end. He promised me a lift back to London on his scooter, and I crawled into his sleeping bag and cuddled up. I could feel his heart beating. I knew we had a connection but it didn't make the sex feel any nicer. He was gentle and slow while he was groping me, feeling my nipples and running his hand down my body between my legs. He was rubbing my bits trying hard to help me enjoy it, but I couldn't. He kept asking me if I was okay. *Okay?* I wondered. *What is okay?* I had left my body as usual, left it for him to take what he wanted, which he did. I had no control. I couldn't stay even if I wanted to; sex meant I had to leave my body and my mind would go to my safe place. I did it all the time and learnt how to get there quickly.

The journey back to London was cold on the back of the scooter. I hugged Greg even though it really was not looked on as cool to hold on to the front rider. It was much cooler to hold onto the back of the seat with your hands behind your back or to just put your hands on your knees. But on this occasion I held on, wishing things could be different and the next Bank Holiday would hurry up and arrive. I felt deflated, knowing I was going back to the world of normality.

Chapter II

The London traffic was jammed, slowly edging forward. Although we were on Greg's scooter, we skipped around a few cars but didn't get far. It was so packed and slow getting to Shepherds Bush that Greg said he couldn't stay and have a coffee in a café. I tried to delay the moment of being left alone. His mates where there waiting on their scooters, and it would have been totally wrong to kiss me in public to say goodbye. He winked at me and said thanks for a great time, revved up his Lambretta engine and raced off with his mates. It sounded like a bunch of giant hairdryers riding down the road.

I was lost, totally lost and alone. I had massive feelings of isolation. *I have no-one, and no-one cares if I live or die,* I thought. London was a big place to hide in; I had no idea where I was, only somewhere in London? Or what I was doing there? So I went into the nearest record shop and looked at flyers for upcoming gigs. Luckily two days was all I had to wait until the next mod gig, *"Pheeew."* As luck would have it the picture on the flyer caught my eye. A target with an arrow through told me it was for mods.

I spent two days wandering around London, riding trains and sitting in bus stations watching the hustle and bustle of the capital as it swallowed people up in its gaping vastness. Greg had given me a tenner and that was all I had to see me through until the gig. I slept in a park on a bench, keeping one eye open and hearing every sound that was made. I drifted in and out of naps waking up to hear a girl's voice.

"Hiya, you don't see many modettes around here. Have you recently moved here?"

I was pleasantly surprised to see another modette standing in front of me holding onto a red Boxer dog. It was keen to go for its walk jumping all around in an attempt to get off the lead. She ignored its pleas after yanking it hard and telling it to, "Behave!"

Girls into mod stuff were pretty rare. I looked her up and down judging her clothing and sense of style. She actually looked pretty good in her blue ski pants and matching sleeveless top. She had on some gorgeous shoes, winkle pickers but flats. They had a large buckle at the side; I hadn't seen any like that before.

We sat in the park for hours and just clicked somehow. I explained my story, for once in my life telling the truth, *well some of it*. I said that I had run away and I had nobody and nowhere to go. Luckily she offered me her couch, saying her parents were away on holiday and that there was just a neighbour looking out for her.

I couldn't believe my good fortune when we arrived after a short bus journey. Walking up a small side road we were in posh London, all detached houses with big bay windows. Her house had a porch that was almost the size of dad's kitchen. *Must be rolling in cash,* I thought. I spent about an hour in the bath soaking the weekend in Scarborough out of my skin. If felt great to get the dirt, sweat and sand out of my hair along with the residue of sex. She showed me a selection of her clothes and offered me a change while mine got washed and dried. It just so happened we were similar in size. I actually felt human for a while.

We sat and talked about my weekend away and how cool it was. She was gutted, telling me she wasn't allowed to go on rallies, but as her parents were away she pleaded with me to take her to the gig that night. She even paid for me to get in. I allowed her to follow me around while I eyed up the talent in the club and looked for who would be dishing out the pills. She fed off of my confidence and seemed to like my superior attitude. As I approached a lad someone grabbed my arm. I turned around and couldn't believe it. It was Gary from Scarborough. Visions of me lying on the beach half naked sprang to mind.

He asked, "What happened to you? I was totally smashed and can't remember much. But I do remember you." He gave me a big double–wink.

I bet you do! I thought. "Sure you do," I said sarcastically.

I was so stoned at the rally, I'm not sure what happened. Gary might well have used and abused me, but funnily enough, it didn't stop me going home with him and his friends. I lost my new friend altogether; I didn't even wonder where she had gone. I was out of my head on pills and vodka. The saying "I was anybody's" couldn't have been truer.

I woke up the next day totally oblivious. The house was empty, apart from a note and £5. The note read, "You were great!" *Oh shit!* I thought. *What did I do?* I stood up and a warm feeling gushed down my legs. The left over's from Gary'--and who knows--night of fun was running down my legs in a sticky mess. Actually, I felt pretty normal. To anyone else it would have been disgusting and dirty! To me it was déjà vu. *It's just what blokes do,* I was still telling myself. I didn't care. I was now all grown up, 14 years old and doing what I wanted in London, no grownups bossing me around and no money either. I had little choice. I could sell myself every night or go home. I came to the decision that although I needed funds, I wasn't going to sell myself so. If I went home I could steal enough to get me away for good. That would allow me to live in my dream-world where I was in control.

With the £5, I made my way to my aunt's house on the other side of London. I have no idea how I found it. I hadn't been there for years, but somehow I did. I was welcomed with open arms and told I could stay there if I wanted and for as long as I wanted. But I knew I had to go home and face the consequences. She phoned dad and arranged for me to be collected at the weekend.

Alex was pretty envious, as I told him about the scooter rally in Scarborough and how I had been to gigs in Shepherds Bush. Riding around on scooters in London, smoking, drinking, drugs, sex, being free, yup, I can safely say he was jealous. Okay I left out the bit about sex to my brother, but it was in my mind. But then he was doing well in his exams and had just been on a school trip to Belgium. I would have chosen MY adventure over his any and every day of the week, but I had to pretend to be interested.

I returned to school the next day to be greeted with a summons to the headmaster's office. My appearance was not one of a girl conforming to society. I was wearing a short black miniskirt, pointed stiletto shoes and had my black bitch-lined eyes and hair done, back combed and sprayed into place with half a can of hairspray, not a strand out of place.

"This will change," he yelled at me crashing his fist on the desk. "You are useless. You will amount to nothing if you do not make an effort."

I calmly listened to him lecture me for awhile before agreeing that I would try and make an effort. "If you say so," I whispered sarcastically under my breath when his back was turned, *Tell me something I don't know,* I thought. I was to be put on report and my behaviour would be monitored. I didn't think it would achieve much, but he had to be seen doing something, didn't he?

I wasn't making friends at school. To be honest I wasn't interested in any of them. Sheila was a bit of a hard nut; everyone avoided upsetting her. No one argued with her and if they did they would be sorry. She came from a well known and feared family, the whole lot of them were well known to the police too. If you messed with her then you messed with her family. Sheila was a well built girl, not very pretty but very popular. Everybody wanted to be her friend, the much safer option.

I had just finished getting my report card signed. I had been to school for three full days on the trot, a small miracle. I was on my way for a cigarette when I felt a shove in the back. I didn't even look, I just spun around fists at the ready and punched whatever or whoever was stood in front of me. It was Sheila!

"Fight... fight... fight..." kids were shouting, as my hair was being pulled out, fists and feet flying. It was quite a cat fight. I gave as many good punches as Sheila did. It took four staff members to separate us. She didn't hurt me. I remember thinking, *Wow! Fighting doesn't really hurt!*

"After school at the old sheds," she spat at me as we were dragged apart. "You better be there."

"Count on it," I said with a really pleased smile.

I did enjoy a good fight. We spent the rest of the day being separated, and I spent the majority of time in with my year head. For a teacher she seemed to have a pretty good clue about where I was coming from. She seemed to understand me, which not many other people could say.

"Don't go and meet her," she said as the bell went. There was a tone of pleading in her voice and I wondered why on earth she cared.

"You know I have to," I said without looking back. I walked out of the school gates and towards the old sheds. A group of kids were following me jeering, shouting and singing, "You're gonna get your fuckin' head kicked in!"

Inside I was smiling, I thrived on the adrenaline rush. I was looking forward to this one. As I turned the corner there must have been thirty kids waiting with Sheila. Not one of them was there supporting me. They daren't because that would mean they were against Sheila.

"You actually showed up," she seemed shocked to see me.

"Why wouldn't I?" I laughed.

"You are the one and only person to ever stand up to me," she said and she smiled. "It was a good fight too," she laughed. "Fag?" She offered me a cigarette and we sat down on the ground and laughed about the whole thing. The crowd of school kids bitterly disappointed that there was no bloody girl-fight to entertain them, started to disperse. We were best mates after that day. I was the only person around who genuinely wasn't scared of her. But I certainly wouldn't recommend fighting wearing a miniskirt!

We looked total opposites. She had her head shaved off apart from her fringe and bits at the sides and bottom of the neck. She hung around with skinheads, wearing tight jeans with braces and black 17 hole Doctor Martin boots. I was a mod and very classy looking compared to her. *My opinion*, I thought, *probably not hers*. We had to be careful not to be seen out together especially at night. Our friends would not have of been impressed and we would have been considered traitors. We managed to remain good friends for at least a year, until the day the Funfair came to town.

The funfair was the highlight for a lot of the locals, mostly it was throwing darts at a board or hooking a duck in a pond. There weren't many fast rides but plenty of opportunity to win a teddy if you picked the lucky ticket and plenty of opportunity to buy candyfloss or fudge.

Punks and skinheads were everywhere. Most of them knew me via Sheila and left me alone. In fact I dabbled in various drugs with a few of them. I was surprised when, above the sound of screaming from kids on the rides, I was ordered to go into the woods to meet Sheila by a few of her friends. I knew I would be meeting her later, but not for a while yet. My guard was up as I felt very wary. I didn't trust these guys, ever! As we neared a clearing I heard Sheila's voice. She sounded upset, pleading to be left alone.

I asked my escort, "What the hell is going on?"

"She's being punished," he said with a smirk in his grin. He looked over to where Sheila was laying on the ground.

"For what?" I enquired making my way over to her. "And get the fuck off her!" I screamed.

Sheila was crying and gagging for breath. One of the male skinheads was kneeling on her with his knee up across her throat and the other on her chest, holding her down.

"For hanging around a stinking fuckin' mod." He laughed and shoved me towards his friends that where waiting in the clearing. I was pushed around by three skinhead guys. They shoved me from one to another like a rag doll and for a moment I feared for my life. I needed to get away and fast. Poor Sheila was pleading for them to leave her alone, at which point another guy shot forward and hit her with a stick the size of a baseball bat.

He shouted, "Shut the fuck up bitch!"

The cracking sound of that limb making contact with Sheila's head made me wince. I heard something break, but I didn't know if it was her head or the stick. It distracted the other two long enough for me to make a break and run for it. I ran like a wild antelope as fast as my legs would carry me. I could hear footsteps running behind but no-one caught me, well not until I had reached the fair ground and was fighting for my breath. I somehow managed to scream for help gulping air. Several members of the public who I had never met came running to my aid.

"Are you okay?" one man asked as others gathered.

Hell no, I'm not okay! I'm about to have a heart attack. And Sheila.

"In the woods. . ." I gasped, pointing. "They're. . .killing. . . her." I was still breathless, I had run so far. Once I managed to explain in more detail, a few guys went to find her.

Before I knew what was happening, an Ambulance arrived and Police were asking questions. They brought Sheila out on a stretcher. Her head and face had been beaten, most probably with that stick or a Doctor Martin boot or two. She was in hospital for two weeks and didn't go back to school for over two months. We both decided it might be safer not to be friends. So that's how it was. We would say hi, nod and smile, maybe talk on the telephone, but it didn't last long. We had a mutual respect for each other and left it at that.

Chapter 12

I met Dave when I was walking home one day from town. It was a long walk, an uphill slog all the way ending in a really steep bit to get to my house. It seemed to take ages and every step left my calves with a burning sensation. I was totally unfit and getting a cramp. Chatting with a friend leaning against the railway bridge at the top of the hill, I caught up with gossip and took a breather. I wasn't far from home when this mod guy wandered up just to say, "Hi." That was the thing with mods, they were friendly to their own local gangs but, of course, far too good for anyone else. Rival gangs most often fought tooth and nail, mods fighting mods. *Really stupid,* I thought, *and all in the name of image or territory.*

I stood there thinking, *How do I look? Is my hair okay? How are my eyes and my bitch lines?* I was wearing pale blue ski-pants and a blue and white sleeveless top with swirly patterns. I had pointed flat shoes with a small buckle on the front. To be honest, I looked more than passable, but I had to go through the motions.

"Are you new to the area?" I asked very curiously because talent like this didn't normally slip through undetected.

"Yeah, just been posted here. What's the local mod scene like?"

"Well, uh. . ." I was staring. "So who. . .uh, what do you. .?"

"I'm in Juniors Leaders in the army. Stationed at the barracks just up the hill."

"No kidding?" It was all that came to mind.

"Would you show me around?" he asked.

Would I ever? Too right! I started to stutter but finally got it out without loosing my calm pretence, "Sure."

This guy was totally fit. He was cool and he spoke with a soft Yorkshire accent which I found very inviting. He was about six feet tall and pretty big built. He played rugby for the Juniors Leaders and had also played for the Yorkshire Juniors I later discovered. So he was a real hunk, well toned too.

Dave was stationed near Folkestone and would be there for six months training. It didn't take long before we started seeing each other on a regular basis. We would meet up at a café in town where all the mods hung out. They had a great jukebox full of oldies and they served wicked bacon butties.

Dave had a scooter which we rode around posing and getting into trouble. I was still stealing and smoking. Dave was always very sensible and tried to talk sense into me, advising me against this or that. At times he got pretty boring to be honest. I tried it all, Purple Hearts, Acid, even glue sniffing and aerosols, anything for a buzz. It really didn't matter. Dave never touched the stuff, and I never did it when he was around. He didn't even drink, never mind do drugs. I didn't feel like I needed drugs when I was with him.

I was falling for Dave hook, line and sinker but, at the same time, I was scared. I figured sooner or later he would want sex. They all did at some point, and I wasn't wrong, After about three weeks of seeing him we were walking up the lane towards the army camp when he pulled me around and started kissing me. He was so passionate! I had never been kissed like that before. I had never actually enjoyed kissing either. The thought of someone's tongue down my throat disgusted me, but this? It was nice, very nice. I never had the power to say "No," even if I wanted to.

"Shhh, your gonna wake them up," I giggled. I had been grounded yet again but it wouldn't stop me from having a good time. If I couldn't go out, then Dave would have to come and sneak in. I sent him around the back to find the ladder propped up against the garden shed. He brought it round to the front of the house and positioned it under my window, scraping the walls. I was giggling and waving at him, "Shhh,Shhh!"

The windows were wooden and heavy, but they slid upwards giving Dave enough room to climb in. In a fit of giggles, we both dived on my bed and lay there talking for hours.

We spoke about our pasts. Dave had had a happy childhood. He had brothers he looked up to and wanted to impress. His birth parents were still together. My story was a wee bit different. I was very insecure. I had begun to hate the world for what it had done to me, and I was well old enough to know what happened to me as a kid was so wrong. I could still feel the pain whenever I thought about it. Somehow though, it never seemed wrong to have sex. I had become very promiscuous. It wasn't hard to get me into bed, in fact, who needed a bed? Sex was sex. I was quite skilled and I knew how to perform because I had been taught from childhood.

I never ever enjoyed it though. I saw guys enjoying it and girlfriends talking about sex with sparkles in their eyes. They talked like they had been reading a Mill's and Boon novel, all mushy stuff that made you want to put your finger down your throat and make yourself sick. *What's so good about sex?* I thought. You lay there writhing around for a bit, moaning and pretending to enjoy it like the ladies in the videos. If he wasn't pounding you, maybe you'd suck his prick and he would cum and shoot sticky stuff in your mouth or on your face, then it was over. Wham Bam, big deal!

I started telling Dave about my past when I heard Maggie stirring. She was coming down the hallway, the floorboards creaking as she made her way to my room. Dave dived under the covers and I pretended to be asleep as Maggie popped her head in my room. Lucky for me she didn't turn the light on. I don't know why she didn't as I'm sure I giggled. My stomach was fit to burst from holding in the laughter, the pains were so real. I really needed to laugh out loud, but if Maggie caught Dave in my room he would be banned. A lot of guys got banned from seeing me. Most of them were wimps and usually did as my Dad or Alex said. Dad and Maggie didn't really like any of the guys I brought home. You would have thought the excitement of nearly getting caught would have been too much for Dave. But no, he hung in there. We had sex in my room that night as quietly as possible. Being scared to wake anyone, it was a bit of thrill if nothing else.

Alex was sleeping in the room right next to me, and I certainly didn't want him woken up. He was getting a bit of a reputation as a hard nut. You didn't mess with Alex and if you did, you thought about it twice the next time. I would go out to mod gigs and Alex would warn guys off me. He was getting pretty boring to be around spoiling the attention I was getting. But he liked Dave and they started to become good friends. Mods liked to hang around Alex because he was cool. He dressed to impress and was never short of a girlfriend. He had a coolness about him people on the mod scene respected.

But because he would cramp my style, I started going out less and less with Alex and more and more on my own. We started growing apart. I was getting fed up taking the blame for him anyhow, alcohol, fags, phone bills. I always accepted the blame and said it was me. Maybe that's why I felt totally unwanted. I was forcing Dad and Maggie to dislike me and I didn't even realise it.

I was pissed at Alex stealing my friends. *Why can't he find his own damn friends?* I wondered. *Why's he stealing mine?* I was very jealous of the way Dad and Maggie treated Alex. *I'm the hero, or is it the martyr?* At least that was how Alex should have seen it. The way he repaid me was by cramping my style. *Thanks Bro!*

Chapter 13

"You're just a slut!" Maggie shouted with her Welsh accent. She always sounded broad Welsh when she was angry.

"For fuck sake, it wasn't my fault. We had to stop for an accident," I tried to explain. I was twenty-five minutes late.

In a shrill laugh she threw at me, "Do you honestly think I would believe anything that came out of your dirty mouth? You wouldn't know the truth if it smacked you between the eyes." She sounded like she wanted an argument, and it began to get more and more heated.

I heard Dave ride off. Otherwise I would have run after him and jumped on the back of his scooter. Instead I had to stand there and face the music. Ironically, we actually did witness a car accident and waited until the ambulance and police arrived.

"All you have to do is call the police, about the accident."

"Sure," she said, "based on your word?"

She refused to listen. She never listened to me. Now, if it was Alex, he could say the moon was made out of cheese and she would believe him. As much as I tried to persuade her to ring the police she would only call me names. I was fuming inside and I saw red. We had done our best to get home on time. For once it wasn't my fault, but I was getting spoken to like I was a piece of shit.

"You're just a whore," she dug deeper, trying to hurt me and succeeding.

Before I realised what was happening, I completely lost it. My brain exploded! I threw myself at her with fists flying, hitting her over and over. *Who does she think she is? She's not my mother!* All she was to me was another bit of fluff Dad brought home and dumped on us. She was dad's new flavour of the month. He always expected us to accept our new mother. Well, Alex might be okay with it, but I wasn't.

"You're not my Mother! Who do you think you are trying to tell me what to do? Just fucking leave me alone!" I yelled. She stayed in the kitchen whilst I was throwing a tantrum, trying to calm me down. She had pushed me too far this time.

I reached my limit and all self control was gone. I ran upstairs to my room and began to panic. *What did I do?* I flung myself face-first beating my pillow senseless. Before I knew it I had fallen asleep, and it was morning, a new day.

Inside I knew I had done wrong. Poor Maggie had always tried her best, but she made it plain she didn't like me, and the feeling was mutual. People would feel sorry for her when she told of how the rebellious teen was wrecking her life.

If only she knew what I've been through, I thought. *She has no concept of having a life wrecked. She should step into my shoes for a day.*

Dad walked in the door on Friday night, as usual. Maggie had already told him what happened on the telephone. He walked straight up to me and smacked me around the face. My cheek burned as I was gobsmacked, literally! Dad had never hit me before, ever! I knew he was angry. He also made it clear that if he was forced to choose between Maggie and me, I would be the loser.

It wasn't nice knowing where I stood, knowing he would choose his latest bit of stuff over his daughter. It was painful, too painful. I was in bits inside, the only bit of stability I had was knowing my dad loved me. Now I just felt like a burden and a hindrance. I suppose it should have been obvious, but I thought I was daddy's little girl. My mind reeled. *Where did I go wrong?*

It was just a matter of time. As soon as I was old enough, I'd be gone. *I won't bother him anymore,* I thought. I felt I wouldn't have been with him at all if his family hadn't bullied him into it. That thought hurt. I began to stay away weekends more often than not, but in order to feed my habits I needed funds. So I stole more of Maggie's money and personal stuff to sell. I would also go into town and steal whatever I could. Naturally, I got caught stealing a few times but always managed to turn on the crocodile tears, flutter my eyelashes, and the managers would let me go on a promise not to do it again.

One Monday afternoon though, the guy in the pawn shop was giving me a weird look while examining the rings. He had never complained or questioned me before, but this time I had a weird feeling. My face started to flush red-hot. My heart was beating so hard I could feel it throughout my whole body. *Does he know they're stolen? How can he tell?*

He looked carefully at the wedding band. Straining to read the inscription he put a magnifying glass over it. I was so stupid, I didn't even know there was a date and initials inside.

"You'll not get much for this, it's marked." He glanced over in my direction and then nodded towards his office. "I just need to go and weigh it, I won't be long," he murmured as he walked away.

He was a tall man, really thin. His shirtsleeves were rolled up exposing black, hairy arms with a ship tattoo on his right forearm. *Maybe he was a sailor,* I thought. His face was long and his features sharp. He had high cheek bones and dark brown eyes, drooping in a tired look.

He was taking longer than usual and I felt uncomfortable alone in the pawn shop. Thinking how easy it would be to steal stuff, I thought, *I could be rich, all this gold and diamonds!* There were glass cabinets all around the shop, some with jewellery inside and other cabinets with ornaments. The counter had watches and bracelets under a glass shelf on one side of the till, and an earring case on the other.

I looked around to see if there were any two way mirrors or anything that would give me away. I was about to grab some stuff when I saw a police car draw up. Adrenalin started to pump as I stared at the front door wide-eyed. I had been caught red handed trying to sell stolen goods. I looked around quickly to see if there was another exit. Nothing, I resigned myself to being caught.

The man walked back out of his office and looked straight at me. I could see the pity and sorrow in his eyes, but he didn't say a word, just opened the door to the police. He explained what had happened and then showed the young policeman my stuff. *Why don't I run?* I could have so easily gotten away. For some reason though, I was frozen in place. Shocked maybe that I had been grassed on, maybe I wanted to be caught.

The policeman was quite nice to me. He guided me into his car with a hand on my arm. His partner made sure I didn't hit my head on the door-frame getting in as we set off for the Police station. I remember thinking how young the policemen were and that I was dating guys not much younger. Looking out the window, I wondered if anyone saw me. I remember thinking it was clever, and how I felt proud to be in a police car again. It was considered something to boast about within my circle of friends.

The officer at the front desk was no stranger. I had been visiting the police station for several months now, usually for stealing, a few times for being in a stolen car and occasionally for fighting. We were becoming familiar to the extent I knew them by first names. In hindsight though, they were just being friendly.

I looked around the cold waiting area at the benches bolted down to the Parquet flooring and the posters on the wall. "Wanted, information on the whereabouts of . . ." There were lots of different posters from missing pets or lost children. I thought, *How long will it be before I'm posted on the wall of fame?*

Of course, I knew it wasn't really clever, but it didn't put me off stealing or fighting. I knew the cells well. I'd been there often enough lately, even signed my own name and dated it, scratching it on the wall with the buckle off my cardigan.

The officer bought me a sandwich and a drink and told me I'd pushed things too far this time. Anyone would think I had robbed a bank the way they were carrying on.

"Getting charged?" I screamed. "Charged for what?"

I knew it was serious but I didn't realise or particularly care what "getting charged" was before then. I could feel my blood boil. I started screaming at the police, "Let me go!" and, "Ring my dad!" I tried the cell door but it was locked. At that point I felt like I had come to the end of the line. I had gotten away with far too much and now I had to pay.

"Your parents aren't interested," the policeman said. He looked pleased. His lip curled at the corner with a small smile forming under his moustache. *Funny,* I thought, *all the police seem to have moustaches?* No one had ever shut me up as quickly as that before.

"We need to go over your statement again before Court," he said calmly. He motioned towards the door and led the way to the interview room.

"Court? Fuck!" I mumbled. I really had pushed it this time.

"What do you mean not interested," I said with a nervous laugh. I walked behind him to the interview room. I thought they were maybe trying to teach me a lesson the hard way, but a part of me sensed he was telling the truth. I didn't argue but needed clarification.

"What do you mean?"

"You've gone too far young lady, trying to sell your mum's wedding ring."

"Oh my god!" I gasped. "I didn't realise it was a wedding ring, really I didn't." *Okay,* I thought, *I can be a bitch but I'm not that bad, am I?*

Albert came into see me at the Police station. He was a Social Worker. He explained that because I was only 15, I needed looking after. He explained how due to my destructive behaviour, my family had given up on me.

"Given up?" I repeated.

"That's right," he said.

"Well, I gave up on them years ago. It's no big deal to me." Inside, my guts were killing me, churning. I was genuinely frightened. Did they really not want me anymore? I wasn't too surprised after hearing dad say he would choose Maggie. *Well who can blame them?*

I had become a rebel, and no one wants a rebel. In fact even before I was a rebel, I didn't think I mattered. As I got older I realised more and more how people around me just wanted to use me or hurt me. I realised then I had no one, no one I could trust, not one person on Earth I could turn to.

I went through my mental list of friends. *Who is important to me?* When I thought about it only two or three actually came to mind.

I sat in the interview room wondering what was going to happen to me. *And, where the hell is Dave? What did they tell him?* He was supposed to pick me up after school on his scooter. He was probably the only person who cared about me. I loved it when he collected me from school. Kids would stand and watch as I hitched my miniskirt up high and slid onto the back of his scooter. I would hold on to the back of the pillion seat, feeling totally cool and important as he pulled off, making sure he didn't rush too much, so that everyone would get an eye-full.

I thought back to the night before last when we walked through the cricket ground and had the bright idea to stay out the night. We broke into the cricket pavilion. It wasn't hard as the wood was old and tired. It only took one firm shove and we were in.

The place smelt of mould. I don't think it had been used for a while. There were pictures around the walls of teams of cricketers proudly holding trophies. In the corner of the room was a glass trophy cabinet and it was locked. I turned and walked towards another room. *Exciting,* I thought. *Wonder what's behind the next door?* It was a kitchen complete with cooker. I fiddled with the knobs but nothing worked. It led into another room with a couch. I could feel the carpet starting to squelch under my feet. No wonder no one was using this place, it was leaky. It stank of mould and damp, but it was fun investigating.

"Let's sleep here tonight." I giggled at Dave throwing myself down on the sofa. *At least it's dry,* I thought, having a good feel of it.

"You're kidding." He did not look amused. "Here? In this shit hole?"

"Oh go on," I pleaded, "You know you want to."

I tried being sexy but it was hard when the place stank of mould and the wallpaper was on its way down, peeling in some places and bubbling in others with a black patch growing up the walls. I knew he wouldn't be able to resist my charms. It was getting late and dark and it was hard to see anything. Luckily no one had seen us break in.

"Let's get some food and come back here," he suggested. I knew he couldn't ever say no when a promise of sex was on offer.

Fish and chips filled the room with a different smell, a nice one. If you couldn't see you might have guessed it was actually home. We lay on the couch eating our dinner. Dave would probably get in trouble with the army again. I was always getting him in trouble encouraging him to stay out, making him late for his duties. He grabbed me closer and gave me a kiss, his tongue searching in my mouth. I could taste the mints he had eaten after the fish.

I knew he loved me, he told me so. Unzipping his trousers he gently pushed my head down. I knew what to do, I had done it plenty of times with Uncle Joe. I never said no. I went into my machine mode and just got on with it. There was never any enjoyment in it, even though I knew he liked it. I suppose I did it to keep him happy. It seemed to work. He pushed me down onto my stomach and put his dick inside me from behind. I don't think he cared if I enjoyed it. We did it, then it was done, nothing major. I couldn't see his face, all I could do was go to my place until it was over. It was nothing memorable.

It rained that night. I heard drips all night long coming in the building and splashing on the floor. *If they condemned this place*, I wondered, *why haven't they taken the trophies out of the cabinet?* If I had won them, I would care more than they did.

We woke up early to birds singing, both of us with frozen fingers and toes. I snuggled into Dave for warmth but he jumped in shock with my ice cold fingers. He shot off the couch obviously not in a very good mood. I'd waken him up. I huffed around and childishly stormed out of the cricket pavilion. *Stuff him, he can get lost for all I care.* I had things to do, and I didn't have time for arguing.

The policewoman interrupted my daydream. "Here, eat this," she said.

She had bought me a bacon sandwich. They kept me there another day saying I couldn't leave until I had been to Court. Albert arrived carrying a bag of bits he had been handed by Maggie outside the Police station. The bag contained a change of clothes, black ski pants and a black and white checked sleeveless top and my makeup bag. *What a blessing!* I spent ages in the toilet, getting dressed and re-doing my backcombed bob and my liquid black bitch lines, my trademark. Finishing off with black clip-on button earrings, I was ready for anything.

I was feeling quite human when we left for Court. The Court building was not far from the Police station and was accessible by an underground passageway. We went that way because it led straight off of the cells area. It took us only five minutes to walk there. I was escorted by two policemen and my social worker, Albert. I remember not being very nervous, though I did wonder when someone was going to jump around a corner and shout, "Surprise!"

Part of me wished someone would, just to cheer everyone up, but it never arrived. This was no joke, soon enough it all started to feel very real indeed. The tunnel stretched on for what seemed miles, the walls looked moist with condensation and, although the bricks had been painted cream, you still knew you were underground. There was a cold draft too. I wondered if I would ever see daylight again.

"Okay, okay, I have learnt my lesson, now please just take me home." I pulled at Albert's jacket as we walked up the stairs into the Court.

"Sorry love, it's not up to me. I'm just here to look after you," he said in his soft Welsh accent. It was the first time I realised he was Welsh. He was such a lovely man, far too nice for this job.

The Clerk of the Court sat at a desk by the main entrance. He had a list of names. Mine was third on the list, Albert checked me in. It told him who I was and where I had to be at what time.

He directed Albert to a side room. I was taken into a small room with closed blinds. I didn't have a clue what was going on. There were a lot of comings and goings, people dressed in suits all lecturing me and telling me to just admit that I had done wrong.

"It would be a lot less painful in the long run," they suggested. Sitting alone in the room, I was bored to tears thinking about Claire again and remembering a few days back when we met up.

We had arranged to go horse riding up the valley. She lived nearby and could see the horses from her window. We didn't know who they belonged to, but it really didn't matter. I borrowed some of Claire's clothes explaining how I had stayed with a friend and hadn't been home to change. I think she knew it wasn't the truth, but she didn't question me. Claire was a bit like me in some respects; she rebelled a lot and knew not to give me an earache. She was similar in size, but not very graceful, very butch in her mannerisms. She always had her bleach-blonde hair cut short and didn't wear much makeup.

The walk up the valley was hard. It was so steep my calves were burning. The thought of riding kept us going though, giggling and laughing all the way. We climbed the fence and caught the first two horses in the field. They were so friendly and just walked right up to us wanting to be petted. With head collars made of bits of rope, we lead them to a nearby fence, climbed on their backs, and off we went.

Riding horse's allowed me a feeling of liberty. Galloping across the field bareback with no tack but a homemade head-collar, I was truly free. I could feel the horse with my legs and sense its intentions. It was like some kind of primordial urge to tame the beast. I pretended to ride like an Indian chasing buffalo or a cowboy flying out of town with a bag full of bank money.

"Yiiipeee!" I screamed, waving my free hand like a rodeo queen.

I rode a Dunn horse, an absolute beauty, and it was massive. I felt like a little girl again, like there was no end to summer and nothing to plan except the next day's ride. Carefree, I beamed with pride to ride well enough to stay on. Sweaty patches on the horse's firm back came from galloping around with a reckless teenager aboard. Of all the shit I had gone through, the sensations of happiness from a bareback ride provided an escape like no other, again and again every time I did it.

For those people like my family, who lectured me on the dangers, riding bareback was foolhardy. "No saddle? No stirrups? How do you stay on?" With balance and anticipation of the horse's response, with an instinct to mould my muscles into its ribs, with a little luck and a lot of practice and patience, that's how. Riding bareback separated the wimps from the brave. No doubt, I was often reckless. I didn't care about my life. I had no sense of danger. Riding without the security of a saddle was like taking drugs, unprotected sex or running with the mods, all a rush of unbridled adrenalin.

I wore the badges of bareback riding--a few visible scars--with pride. The way my legs could completely relax alongside the horse's body, my feet swinging to the same rhythm as its head felt so natural and tantalizing. There was no tension in my body, and my mind was free to explore. And I did. I just disappeared to a nice place, that nice place that only appeared on horseback. I had respect for horses, for their beauty and intelligence. It was the only thing I actually loved with all my heart.

Riding through the forest, jumping broken trees and dodging bushes, I felt like I was floating. When I was on that horse there were no hospitals, no dying mums, no wicked step mothers, no perverted uncles just a thousand pounds of muscle straining to please me. It was a half-ton of living flesh throbbing between my legs, a rush no man could ever give me. On a dead-run, when I was not in full control, I loved every second. Girlie squeals come from my mouth as we raced up the meadow. Laughing out loud, there were no troubles in the world and I forgot everything, absolutely everything!

The horses were soaked in sweat from our reckless riding. I slid off looking at the white foam where the rope had rubbed on her neck. I pulled long, dry grass and rubbed her down. She stood there closing her eyes enjoying the company and the human touch. After a while Claire and I ran off down the meadow laughing and jabbering, all energized after our thrill ride. We didn't give a toss they didn't belong to us. I truly believed we were doing those horses a favour. Without their twice weekly ride, they probably didn't have much human contact. Of all the times we rode them, we were never once challenged by anyone.

"Huh hum," the cough from Albert clearing his throat brought me back to my senses. *Oh shit!* I looked up from where I had been scratching the table in a daydream.

Chapter 14

A massive reality check struck as I remembered where I was. I heard Maggie's voice on the other side of the door, but I was told I wasn't legally permitted to speak to any witnesses prior to the hearing. If I said I wasn't scared. I would have been lying. I was petrified. With the exception of Albert everyone just spoke at me, dictating this or that or having conversations about me as if I wasn't even there.

The building was old. It had marble floors and all the furniture was bolted down. The bookshelves were nailed to the walls too. *Who is going to steal them?* I thought. *They would need a lorry.* The seats were plastic, similar to the ones you find in the school canteen, and they weren't in-keeping with the rest of the building. The old stone, antique wood and marble floors were beautiful. I was sure there must be a reason the chairs were made of plastic. I might have been only 15, but I knew what looked good.

"Vandals," Albert read my mind. "They bolt them down so people can't throw 'em."

"Throw them?" I giggled, as I imagined someone throwing chairs at the Judge while he shouted, "Guilty!" with a plum in his mouth.

In turn my name was called, and Albert stood in the doorway beckoning me to follow. I did so with purpose and pride in my steps. I really didn't give a toss what this Judge said. I just wanted the whole palaver to be over and done with. Or that's the impression I wanted to give.

I had a weekender coming up and there was planning to be done. I was going to Margate to meet up with my mates, and it felt like I hadn't seen them for ages. Dave had taken up quite a lot of my time recently, so I felt like I had neglected the mods. I wanted to make it up to them and go out and have some fun, although Dave was supposed to go along.

The Judge looked pretty normal to be fair, apart from a wig on his head, which he took off as I entered the room. He looked and sounded like a nice guy. There were people on either side of him. It wasn't the type of court I had imagined from what I had seen on TV.

The Judge told me to sit down and various reports were read. Then the witnesses were asked to stand up and were questioned on their written statements. They even had a report prepared by the school. *Of all the nerve,* I thought. *What business is it of theirs what I was doing at school?*

The Judge sat and listened intently, occasionally looking over in my direction. I was yawning and getting totally fed up fidgeting and sighing the whole time, until the Judge called for Maggie. That grabbed my attention.

Maggie walked into the court, looking very smart in a suit. She fit in well with everyone else in suits. As she passed me, she gave me a nervous smile before walking with her eyes fixed on the floor, avoiding the gaze of everyone in the Court. She made her way to the seat where she had been guided by the Court usher. She looked a lot more nervous than I did. *Well, serves her right. If she had collected me from the Police station, we wouldn't be here now would we?* The Judge asked her all about me. How long she and dad had been living together? And, what sort of child I was?

Maggie proceeded down her shit list. She told the Judge of all the things I had done since she had been living with dad: the lying, the stealing, how I would run away all the time and that she quite literally had no control over me. She spoke of the kinds of things she had tried to make me stop. "But, no matter what I tried," she said, "Abbie ignored me." She continued to tell them how I would steal alcohol and cigarettes and disappear for weekends, sometimes longer. She went on to say that she and dad were worried that something serious would happen to me if someone didn't take control. She said she had given me her best shot, but she was done trying and couldn't do any more. "I don't even WANT to do any more," she said in a desperate tone.

My mind was reeling. *When catalogued like that, I sound awful. But what she and the court failed to realise is at least half of what she listed was actually Alex.* At that moment I thought to myself, *If only I had told them sooner.*

What on Earth was Maggie worried about anyway? I knew she was unaware of my true past. Molly was the only person who knew the full extent of what happened to me. If Maggie had known, I was sure she would have picked me up from the station. She certainly wouldn't be in Court saying all these nasty things and making me look like shit.

I kept looking around thinking, *Where is Alex?* Perhaps he hadn't been allowed to attend court. I suspect he wasn't. He had gotten himself a job in a supermarket after school as he wanted money for going on scooter rallies and for drink and drugs. Apparently he didn't steal much at all when I wasn't around. He had become the blue-eyed boy and he wouldn't want to spoil those impressions, so he got a job. I hadn't seen him for ages, just typical of him to not be bothered about my troubles. *Why doesn't Alex ever stand up and take the blame he's due?* But then to be honest, if people really liked to think it was all me, then let them. Let them believe whatever they wanted.

I really didn't care! I was 15 now, totally capable of looking out for myself. Those here in Court obviously felt differently.

Maggie's report continued something like:

"I would often walk Abbie to school to ensure she attended, but as soon as I had turned my back she would change out of school uniform into miniskirts and other inappropriate clothing. She had no respect for anyone including myself and was getting deeper and deeper in trouble."

The Judge asked me to wait outside for a while.

Albert escorted me outside with a worried look and whispered, "Not good."

"Whatever," I responded shrugging and scraping my foot on the floor. There was a small stone that my foot found, and I was pushing it back and forth scraping the wooden floor in the side room. I had had enough. I was tired, and I couldn't be bothered with this crap. I just wanted to get out of here.

I sat back in the little room on my own, while Albert went to fetch a drink. I wasn't allowed out in the public waiting area because I was under 16, but I could hear the voices and all the people coming and going. I thought about running, I knew Albert wouldn't catch me but I also knew I had to get it over with. If it didn't happen today, it would another.

It seemed an eternity before I was finally called back into the courtroom. I passed Maggie on her way out and she was crying.

"I'm sooo sorry," she mouthed at me like I could read lips. *Why is she crying? What does she have to be sorry for? What has she done?*

The Judge asked me to sit down and coldly delivered his speech. "Young lady, for your own safety you are being made a Ward of Court. When your parents refused to collect you at the Police station, Social Services was left with little or no choice but to start the process of handing parental control to a Judge. This means your Social worker has become responsible for reporting your future behaviour. Before you will be allowed back home, your behaviour must improve. For now I will arrange for you to be taken care of."

I almost belted out, *What, like Uncle Joe or the others?* I could feel myself getting angry. *They really had no clue. They wouldn't do anything even if they did. I know they wouldn't!* I was to be taken into care, to a residential home whilst I sorted out my behaviour.

"Ha!" I laughed out loud shaking my head. *What a bunch of pricks, the lot of them.*

Albert assured me it would be "okay" and asked me to calm down. "You can go home when you get yourself sorted out. You just need a little help, that's all."

Where was the help when I was a kid?

I needed to get hold of Dave. *How will he know where to find me? What about Alex?* Albert reassured me he would let everyone know where I was and not to worry, it would all be okay. I had no choice, the police escorted me into his car. I didn't know where I was going or what would happen.

Chapter 15

The children's home was about ten miles from my house. I knew the area but not well. I watched as we passed different roads and junctions while trying my hardest to remember where we had been. We turned into a quiet lane and drove for about one more mile before turning into a large private driveway with a mini-roundabout full of flowers. The lawns were looked after as was the rest of the garden. It looked so tidy, so posh. The gardener popped his head around from a shed door and nodded hello. I just looked at him wondering what went on in his shed.

The house was massive, the heavy, wooden double doors were very impressive indeed. They had stained glass panels either side and a large brass, horseshoe door knocker. Albert rang the bell and a voice called out asking us to come in.

The woman in the hall was up a ladder putting a light bulb in the fitting on the ceiling.

"If you want something done, do it yourself," she called down to Albert. "Staff are bloody useless here." She jumped down and walked towards me hand outstretched to shake my hand.

Pfft! Shake my hand? I laughed. *Does she think I'm a businessman or something?* I offered my hand and she shook it. I don't think I had ever shook hands with anyone before that.

"Jane is my name and I do all sorts around here including changing light bulbs. In fact, I'm pretty much a general dog's body." She nodded towards the light, raised her eyebrows and tutted.

"Follow me, I'll show you around." She led the way with purpose. I felt like she was rushing. *Maybe I'm keeping her from doing other stuff, maybe changing more light bulbs?* On we marched room after room, "This is the dining room," she said. pointing through a doorway. There was a table laid with ten places. *Ten kids?*

"Oh great that's all I need," I murmured to Albert.

He smiled and said, "Behave," in an attempt to sound authoritative.

"Where do I sleep?" I questioned Jane.

"Right at the top of the stairs," she said as she led the way into what looked like the attic. She told me how I had been given my own room because I was one of the oldest there.

Too right, I thought as we climbed three flights of stairs. *Do they really think I would share?* The room next to mine was shared by twin sisters six months younger than me. The rest of the kids slept on the floors below. We had our own fire escape in the attic which was a metal staircase attached to the outside of the building. My room had views over the back garden with nothing very exciting to see. *Unless you like looking at huge fern trees,* I thought. They seemed to have been planted there to prevent neighbours from being nosey. The adjoining properties were totally hidden from sight.

Nothing really exciting to do here, I thought as I turned my attention to my room. A single bed along the wall near the window gave me something to kneel on as I looked out. The bed wasn't made, but it had a pile of sheets and blankets neatly folded at the bottom end. A cream dressing table sat on the facing wall with a small, delicately carved vanity mirror. A wicker chair sat in the corner with a red cushion. There were several pictures on the walls, pictures of puppies and kittens and a forest scene with rabbits. The wall near the door had a full length mirror. I surveyed myself checking out my hair and makeup as a voice beckoned Jane. We made our way back downstairs.

Out of what looked like an office came a young woman about 25 years old. Introducing herself as the manager of the home, her name was Elsie. She stood there and lectured me about house rules, at which point I turned and began walking away.

"Where do you think you're going?" she called after me. Following me, she tried to grab my arm.

"Get the fuck off me!" I screamed in her face, snatching my arm away. "If you touch me again you'll be fucking sorry." I threatened her and meant it. *Who the hell does she think she is?*

"Let's try again," she said. "You're obviously upset."

"Upset? Upset? You don't know the fucking half of it," I said with a lump in my throat. I wasn't about to feel sorry for myself, especially today. I didn't normally so why start now? I pulled myself together quickly so the tears didn't come. I couldn't remember when I last cried, but even then, it was crocodile tears not real ones.

"Come on Abbie, calm down," Albert butted in.

"Abbie, please can we try again?" Jane looked at me pleading and trying a different tactic. It was enough to make me pause and think. I followed her back into the office.

"If all you want to do is lecture me then don't bother," I said as I slumped onto a chair. She nodded and smiled. She looked over to Albert raising her eyebrows as if to say, *We've got a tough one here haven't we?* "Okay then, let's just try one or two rules today shall we? No fighting here and curfew is 9:00 pm."

"You've got to be kidding," I laughed. "I'm not a baby you know. If you think I am coming in at 9:00 pm you've got another thing coming."

I couldn't be bothered to argue. I was tired and upset, so I shrugged my shoulders and said I would try just so I could get away. But I wouldn't promise anything.

Albert stood up as if to leave. I followed him to the door where he handed me a pack of cigarettes and a £5 note. He promised to go straight to the barracks and leave a message for Dave telling him where I was.

"Don't forget," I called after him.

"Don't worry. Just you behave," he winked and smiled back at me.

As I watched him get into his old red Beetle, I knew once again I was alone. I asked Jane where I could smoke and walked out into the garden where I sat and stared into space. I wondered if my dad had ever really cared about me, I mean really, truly cared.

A yellow minibus pulled into the drive. I watched as kids jumped off laughing and looking really happy. Two older girls got off, both had skinhead haircuts. *They are having a fucking laugh,* I thought to myself. *I'm a mod and they put me in a kid's home with skins? Do they want to see fights or something?* I thought to myself remembering the grief I went through with Sheila.

I walked further away down the garden to plan what to do next. I didn't know exactly where I was or how to get hold of Dave, so I thought I had better wait until Albert got hold of him. Then we could sort everything out together. The skinhead girls followed me up to the end of the garden, and I readied myself for a fight. They approached me and asked if I had a spare fag?

"You have got to be fuckin' joking!" I replied sarcastically.

"We don't want trouble," they said, one girl holding her hands up as if to surrender.

"We've got to live together so let's just try and get on shall we?" She was pretty smart really. I wasn't in the mood for trouble.

I felt like I was sinking, like the whole world was swallowing me up. I offered the girls a cigarette, lit it for them and then sat and listened while they told me their life story. Their parents were killed in a car crash and they were waiting to go into foster care. I told them I had been dumped by my dad and his new girlfriend. They thought I was pretty cool to get into so much trouble at my age.

I had them eating out of my hand. They explained that despite the image, they never had the nerve to do the kind of things I did. I began to like them even though they were skins. It felt good to have someone look up to me.

Dinner was served in the dining room, which was full of kids ranging between eight and 15. With the exception of one boy, I was the eldest. I wasn't very hungry and left most of my dinner even though it was my favourite, Bangers and Mash. I went to my room but as yet, I had no clothes to change into. They had offered me some, but I told them I wouldn't be seen dead in them. Albert said he would fetch some from Maggie and deliver them tomorrow. I lay on my bed and wondered what I had done to deserve this? *Why me?*

Don't get me wrong, I didn't feel sorry for myself in that sense, but I was left wondering where it had all gone wrong? I had only just figured out what I went through as a kid wasn't normal. I wasn't really a bad person. I just wouldn't allow myself to be good. It was some kind of self-preservation thing. I enjoyed the attention I got from being a rule breaker. It was my way of fighting back at the treatment I received as a child, unlike Alex, who did his best to hide his emotions.

When I woke up it was light, and there was a knock at the door.

"Get up, come on, wakey wakey," I could hear the voice banging on all the bedroom doors, one after another. I threw the covers off. I hated everything and I was in a bad mood.

"I'm sick of this fuckin' place already! I'm sick of people making me do things and I'm sick of my shit fuckin' life!" I screamed.

I looked up into the mirror as I passed. A voice in my head yelled at me, it was mum telling me all over again. "You're Ugly!" My fist flew at the mirror and it shattered. Little shards of glittering glass flew around me to the floor. The razor sharp pieces cut my skin and my knuckles were bleeding. "Why can't I just die?" I bellowed at the top of my voice. A line of blood trickled down my arm. I threw my fists into the wall causing the pictures to shake.

It hadn't taken long. Once again I was back into my world of hatred and pain. Almost every day I slipped back to my childhood, when my stepmother tortured me for fun and did her upmost to destroy my spirit. From the moment I left the Court and arrived at the kid's home, the feelings of rejection and loneliness built inside of me. My tantrum was the anger coming out. It felt like I had hit rock bottom. I could feel the pain and violence whenever I thought about Sue as if it was yesterday, and I knew that the feelings of anger raging inside of me were because of her.

Looking back, I saw fists coming at me, blood dripping from my nose and ear. She walked patiently around me waiting for me to break down. It was her game. Whenever I spoke of my real mum I was punished. It was her way of controlling me and making me suffer. She would stop hurting me only when she got bored of it. I believed I was worthless, she told me every day. *Who was I to argue?* My thoughts, hopes, dreams and memories of my real mum had been totally beaten out of me. I could control it no longer. It was usually at this point that I wished I could go back in time. If I was there now, it would be her getting the beatings. I imagined myself beating the crap out of her just to let her know what it felt like.

I grabbed the bottle of perfume Dave had bought me, which Maggie had brought to the Court for me to freshen up. I slung it as hard as I could against the door. More jagged pieces of glass flew everywhere. I was shocked when it bounced straight back at me. I threw my hands up to my face and felt the glass showering the back of my hands. Apparently no-one heard the smash, because no-one came. It was my temper and it was aimed at me only. I wiped the cuts on my arm and wrist, pulled down the sleeves to hide my hands and left my room. I felt a whole lot better.

I could smell bacon downstairs and the sound of kids giggling in the room below me. It sounded like a holiday camp, but I had already figured it wasn't. It seemed that every day there were different staff. I learned there were several shifts. Some I got on with and others I didn't, but for the most part we ignored each other.

It was at least five days before Albert arrived with some clothes. Apparently he had been ill. I wore the same two sets of clothes for almost a week. Apology or not, I wasn't impressed and let him know it. Dave had been sent on a last minute exercise with the army the day after I arrived at the children's home. A sigh of relief, *That's why he hasn't been to visit me.* He was due back in three days and would come and see me then. Albert didn't stay long, but gave me more cigarettes and more money in case I ran out while they were sorting out my pocket money allowances.

The days dragged. I would have to start back at my regular school on Monday. They would drop me off in the van and collect me. Part of my care order was education, and so I had to attend school as part of the deal. *If I don't go to school I'll never come off this damn "Ward of Court" crap,* I thought. I was not looking forward to school! I hadn't been there for over two months. I really couldn't be bothered with all the catching up or the constant explanations as to why I had been absent.

I sat in the garden smoking and heard that familiar sound, a bit like a hairdryer, and my ears perked. Dave! I ran around to the front of the house and saw him pull into the drive. I had never been so happy. He was all I had. Even my own brother hadn't bothered to ring me or find out how I was doing. But I knew I could depend on Dave. I ran over hugging him so hard. I knew it was totally not cool to do that in public, but I couldn't resist. I was bursting with excitement!

I turned back and saw the employees watching out of the staff room window as Dave arrived and got off his scooter. He was 17 now and I knew they didn't like the fact I was seeing someone older. One lady came out to remind me of my curfew as I hopped on the scooter and we pulled away.

"Where to my lady?" his Yorkshire accent yelled above the roar of the engine.

"Anywhere but here. How about the beach?" I shouted, hugging him tight. I could smell him through his coat, and it was wonderful just to smell something familiar.

Chapter 16

Dave headed toward the beach in Dover. After about twenty minutes along the coastline, we arrived in the middle of nowhere. It was fantastic to have the wind in my face, to feel free again.

The beach was mostly pebbles, not much sand at all. We hobbled our way over the loose stones towards the sea and sat ourselves on a mound of boulders. It wasn't very comfortable or romantic really, but we sat for about 30 minutes and stared at the sea saying nothing. I studied the waves breaking on the rocks trying to make sense of what the heck occurred over the last couple of weeks. It all happened so fast, I couldn't make sense of it. Dave had his arm around me and suddenly asked me why I had been so stupid? I didn't know what to say. I just always seemed to have the self-destruct switch flipped to ON.

I felt safe and I knew I would be while Dave was around. He was so sensible. We lay back on uneven rocks and I rested my head on his chest. We thought up ways we could be together. Maggie and dad had told him they didn't want him around me for a while. They felt I needed to sort myself out, and they didn't want me back home until I had.

"Well that's a never then," I sighed. "I can't be what they want me to be. I'm not what they want." It was at that moment I realised and said to Dave, "I don't think I will ever be going back home again."

Time was ticking away. I knew I had to be back for curfew, and I didn't want to spoil the first time in a while I had seen Dave. We arranged to meet the next day, exchanging contact phone numbers. I gave him the children's home phone number, and he gave me his friend's house phone number so we could stay in touch.

The next few days started feeling better. Dave was around a lot of the time, much to the annoyance of the home staff. They told me, "Dump him, he's no good for you." They thought he was putting pressure on me all the time. If anything, it was the other way round. I was getting pretty fed up. The staff had left me alone most of the time, but it soon changed when Dave came on the scene again. I told them I would think about it and to "just off my back while I decide what else I can do."

Dave picked me up the next day. It was Saturday afternoon by the time we got away. We rode down the coast as usual, and although Dave was tired having been on guard duty all night, we decided to find somewhere quiet to be together. Sex was high on the agenda but we weren't really that bothered where. We found a disused railway and followed it for a while. We came across an old bridge with a metal gate underneath. Dave looked around and found a metal pole and struggled but managed to wrench the gate apart with it. We seemed to have this uncanny knack of finding really glamorous places to spend time together. I was getting used to these up-market locations for sex. *Why don't we just do it in the dirt,* I thought.

"We don't have much time," he said as he hurriedly took off his green parka and laid it on the ground for me to lie on.

"But, can't we. . ?"

"You don't want to get in trouble for being late," he sounded concerned. I knew what was coming but was totally powerless to resist. I had smoked some happy backie and felt really cosy and relaxed.

When Dave rolled off of me and dozed off after his fierce five-minute shag, I lay there in a world of my own. I could feel the sticky mess oozing between my legs and wondered if he had any tissues. I was blissfully unaware that I was past my curfew. I dozed off too, and when I came to, it was pitch black. Dave was fast asleep and I could hear rustling nearby. It seemed far too loud for a fox or a badger. Had someone found us? Had they been watching us all along? Fear dug in between my ribs. It went silent again for a few minutes then the rustling and moving around got louder. I grabbed Dave shaking him attempting to wake him quietly.

"Sshhh," I whispered into his ear, "there's someone there." My eyes were wide in fear and I was breathing heavy.

"Who's there?" He called out into the trees. It fell silent again.

"It's not fucking funny, now, come out," I shouted into the dark.

Dave grabbed for the metal bar for and we warily tip-toed back to the gate. Scrunch-a-boom! A loud crashing noise exploded in front of us and large tree branches snapped. We both flew back from the gate scrambling and grabbing at each other in the black tunnel straining to see in the dark. Suddenly, a big, black and white cow came through the hedge and stared at us like, *What the hell are you two doing here?*

"Shit!" Dave said throwing the pole into the back of the tunnel in disgust. He muttered under his breath while I burst out laughing. The poor cow ran off into the black of night, charging through another hedgerow. I couldn't stop giggling for ages. I honestly thought it was the boogieman and it was a milk cow.

"My hero," I threw my arm around Dave imagining how he was protecting me.

"Aah shit!" he cursed looking at his watch. "Shit, shit, shit!" was all he could say. "Come on," he said grabbing my arm, more or less dragging me back across the tracks, through the undergrowth to his scooter.

The house was dark, not a light on and not a sound. Dave had stopped his scooter around the corner so he wouldn't draw attention to our arrival. As I sneaked up the metal stairs which led to my room, Dave took off. I hoped and prayed the window wasn't locked, but no luck. Sealed! Alone and totally frustrated and annoyed, I hadn't thought to unlock the window before I left, so I had no choice. I went back downstairs and sat on the door step. I couldn't risk waking everyone so I sat on that cold, hard doorstep until the sun rose in the sky and staff turned up for work.

"Wakey wakey," Jane appeared up the walk. "What happened to you last night? You had everyone worried. They reported you to the police as missing," she said with her back to me, unlocking the front door and picking up the milk bottles. I must have slept through the milk delivery. She walked inside.

"Missing?" I repeated parrot fashion. I pulled myself up off of the doorstep and followed her in. I climbed the stairs to my room, feeling shattered and not caring less if I was in trouble. I didn't want Dave to get in trouble, so I would keep him out of it whatever it took.

I lay on my bed trying to think up some amazing cock-and-bull story that might clear him, but I came up short. No one would believe me for a minute that we had fallen asleep in a tunnel or even that we fell asleep anywhere. No one on Earth was fool enough to believe the cow story. I thought, *See, even when I tell the truth no one believes me so what's the point?* I could feel the anger rumbling inside me like a volcano. I felt cornered. Four members of staff were there telling me how I was grounded, and how I worried everyone sick. Obviously,

Dave couldn't be trusted so I was banned from seeing him ever again.

"Oh, you reckon do you?" I screamed. "Who the fuck do you think you are? You can't tell me what to do! And don't fucking look at me like that or I will wipe that look off your face!"

I was livid, blood boiling, adrenaline rushing through my body like a snort of cocaine. *How will they stop me? They'll have to lock me in my room!* I marched out of the office. Phil followed me out into the hall and put his hand on my shoulder to stop me walking away. I just flipped. I don't know what came over me. I started hitting him, kicking him, and punching for all I was worth. It was seconds, really, before other staff came to his support. Before I knew it I was on the floor being pinned down by four staff members. It took a while before I could feel anything, like the pain in my neck from being kneed to the ground. I guess they had no choice but to protect them and me from myself. Fingers dug into my arms to hold me down and the pain started to get more and more real. I couldn't breathe and my heart was racing, full panic mode.

"Just calm down," a male voice tried to reassure me.

"Get off me!" I screamed shifting to move the bodies. I finally got tired from the struggle and started to give in and calm down. Phil was talking to me softly, trying to calm me down and advising me or rather telling me how this sort of behaviour got me nowhere.

Oh yeah, I thought, *like I had intended to flip out or something.* I didn't want to hurt anyone. It was just a switch that turned on in my head when I got scared. It was the time in my life when my thirst for fighting worsened. Anything was an excuse for a good fight. Kids at the home began to avoid me and I started to rebel even harder.

I would sneak out at night in order to meet Dave. We would find somewhere to go and be together, meeting up with friends in a café or just going for a ride on his scooter. I really didn't care what we did. I was his as long as he got me away from that kid's home.

Chapter 17

I hadn't been to see Maggie and dad for months, and they still hadn't been to see me since I was put in care. Alex was 17 now, and he hadn't bothered with me either. He knew where I was and he had transport. He was far too busy being the good boy, I guess. Dave told me he had seen Alex out quite a lot recently, but Alex was popping a lot of pills so he stayed away from him.

I felt totally abandoned by my family. Dad finally got what he wanted, kids out of his hair. He had Maggie waiting hand and foot on him, and Alex at home occasionally. Of course I was bitter, but there was a part of me that still missed home. I missed little things like cleaning out dad's truck at the weekend and blaring out the radio. I missed seeing dad but I had a "stuff them" attitude. *I don't need them. I don't need anyone. I will just look after myself thanks!*

Dave was away with the army, training for something or another, for several weeks. During that time, I had ran away and been fetched back to the home by the police more than three times. I lost count how many times I ran away or "absconded" as the home staff called it. If I heard of a gig or a weekender off, I went. I didn't give a toss if I was allowed to or not.

"Just give me my own place!" I would whine in meetings with the home and social workers. "I'm not a kid anymore, so stop trying to treat me like one." Month after month I sat through the same meetings, mapping my future. Strangers decided what they thought was best for me. *How can they know what's best for me when they don't even know me?* All they knew was what they had read in a file.

The following Saturday evening arrived and the staff were well aware that I wanted to go out clubbing. I couldn't contain the excitement I felt at the prospect of going to this particular gig. It promised to be a good one. I had let slip about it during our meeting and been told, "No, under no circumstances will you be allowed to go!"

I knew Dave was back today and he would be there waiting to see me. The night staff had just changed shifts and Phil was on with Anna. I had missed Dave so much and was looking forward to seeing him. I spent hours getting ready. My hair was freshly dyed black and had been cut into a fresh five point Quant style bob. It was slightly backcombed and sprayed heavily into place. My skin was white with pale foundation. I had used white eye shadow and thick, black liquid liner to do my trademark bitch lines. The look was finished off with white lipstick.

I had new underwear too. They had taken me out that day shopping for clothes and underwear and to have new bras fitted. I was growing almost by the day, my boobs were a 38DD. For 15 years old they were pretty big. It helped me get into clubs as most girls at 18 wouldn't have a chest my size. I wore stockings underneath my dress which was my black and white, dog-tooth, checked mini. It had four large, black buttons down the front and I wore black calf boots and a short, black jacket. I was looking good.

On my way down the stairs I met Anna who was on her way up.

"Why are you all dressed up? You're not going anywhere," she said with a sarcastic tone in her voice.

"I beg to differ," I said as I continued down the stairs. She grabbed me and yanked my arm. In a blinding flash I went after her swinging. I could hear Phil shouting stuff at me, but I couldn't make it out and I couldn't stop. Anna was trying to drag me upstairs and before I knew it, she tripped, tumbling head first down the whole flight of stairs. Frozen in place, I was powerless and all I could do was stare. Her body banged off of the wall and off the banisters crashing down in summersaults. Arms extended she pulled pictures off the wall, glass shattering down the stairs. In a blind panic I ran right past her as she finally stopped in a crumpled heap.

I could hear myself shouting, "I'm sorry, I'm SORRY!"

Phil was screaming after me to stop and come back. But I thought I had really done it this time. She was hurt bad. Even though I knew I hadn't pushed her, I knew I hadn't, but who would believe me? *She could even be dead for all I know.*

I made my way to the train station and snuck on as always. I hadn't paid for a train, ever, and had never been caught. The train was packed full of people of all ages. A lot of them were looking at me. *Do they know? Do they know I hurt Anna? Do I have GUILT written all over my face?*

"Who you fucking looking at?" I asked the guy opposite me. He turned red and looked away. "Fucking idiot," I told him as I stood up and walked to the next carriage. That was me at 15, not a nice person at all.

I tried not to think about what had happened at the home and concentrate on the gig. I had been looking forward to it all week. The train ride was about 40 minutes, but all the time my mind was back at the home wondering if I had killed Anna. *Murderer? Am I a murderer?*

The station was busy when I arrived. I felt a little panicky at the thought of not finding Dave among the crowd, but I made my way through the station, doing my best to blend in so I wasn't stopped and asked for my ticket. I needn't have worried. I made my way through the exit double doors and there was Dave sat proudly on his scooter right at the front of the station.

I beamed with joy. I would have loved to run up and give him a huge hug, but that would have been totally un-cool. So we just walked and parked his scooter then wandered around the block and found a quiet place to be near the hall the gig was in.

We found an out-building and went inside. I told him about Anna and he looked concerned but reassured me everything would be okay as he lifted my dress and fingered me before putting his dick in me and having a quickie. I'd love to make it sound romantic, but there was nothing romantic about it. In fact the out building stank of piss and there were cobwebs everywhere. I scanned the walls for moving spiders and relaxed a bit. There was excrement smeared on the walls and bog roll everywhere on the floor soaking up the water and piss on the floor. *Nasty place!*

"Not very romantic," I said as my knickers fell down to my ankles and he pumped his lower body against mine. On high alert in case someone came in and trying my hardest not to let my new knickers touch the floor, I could hear the music in the hall, *Give me just a little more time* by the *Chairmen of the Board*. I thought about the great timing and how ironic those lyrics were. Lots of people were laughing and talking outside. It was over very quickly as usual. I patted my dress down, pulled my knickers up and we went back into the gig and danced to 60's and soul music. I popped more pills trying to forget about Anna and not caring what I was doing to my body.

The hall was full of mods and scooterists drinking and having fun. A lot of girls were dancing. The lads were outside as usual comparing scooters and admiring paint jobs, working out how many mirrors could be attached to one scooter, and who had the best fox's tail attached to the aerial on the back. Before I knew it the night was over. It had been a great time but not worth killing someone for. My foggy mind went back to the home to think about what would happen when I returned.

We arranged to meet the following week. I told Dave that the home didn't want us to be together anymore and they were doing their best to separate us. We sat and made plans to run away together. He was going to run away from the army for me. He wanted to be with me forever. He said he loved me and that we would work it out.

When I got back it turned out the Anna wasn't dead at all. Luckily, she was only bruised. I kept quiet for a few days thanking my stars for the lucky escape. *What if?* The thought sent chills down my spine.

Chapter 18

Dave had spoken to Alex in the local pub and was told to pass on a message to me that Molly and Kassie were going to visit dad for the weekend. I hadn't seen them for years. In fact I hadn't seen any of the kids. I often thought about them and wondered what they were doing and if they were okay. I often wondered if Molly still had to visit Uncle Joe.

I didn't want Maggie to know that I had every intention of seeing them, so I got Dave to arrange through Alex a place to meet. *Will I recognise them? What will I say?* The thought of seeing them made me feel sick with nerves. It brought a lot of memories back to the forefront of my mind. I thought I had locked some of those scenes away for good. Part of me didn't want to see any of them ever again, the memories far too painful. I could still smell Sue's crotch and feel the panic of not being able to breathe. It seemed like only yesterday.

We met at the park near dad's house and I recognised Molly straight away. She was growing up so fast. *Who am I kidding? She's the same age as me.* Molly ran up to me, hugging me like there was no tomorrow. I didn't think she would ever stop. I looked around nervously to see if anyone saw this outward display of affection. She appeared so ill and thin. It looked like she needed a hot dinner or two. Her eyes were dark underneath, and I could see the pain in her eyes. She smiled, beaming, like she was so pleased to see me. She was maybe two inches taller and a lot skinnier than me. She had short, mousy brown hair and she was quite flat-chested. I was proud of my boobs. They got me a lot of attention. She wasn't pretty at all, her teeth never did get fixed. They were pushing in all directions and I felt sorry for her. Image meant a lot to me and I could see she had no sense of self worth. But then even if she had, it wouldn't have done her any good, mum would never have helped or encouraged her to look pretty.

Alex took Kassie over to the swings and Molly and I wandered off and sat on the football field. For a while we sat there in silence, just looking at Alex playing with Kassie. I guess neither of us knew what to say. Rabbits were running around at the edge of the park, hopping in and around the new flowers and over small logs in spring play. *If only life was that easy and fun,* I thought to myself.

"Have you told anyone?" Molly looked me straight in the eye.

Oh my god! Do my eyes tell the story like hers? Do I look in that much pain?

"No," I said quietly. "No, I haven't told a soul and I don't have any intentions of doing so either. Let's face it, who would believe us anyway?"

"It's our secret, then, no matter what happens." We agreed linking our little fingers together and shaking them up and down in a pinkie promise. It was a pact. We swore that no one would ever know.

We both had seen cases on TV, court cases on the news of people who were paedophiles. We had seen the news of children being abused, of people going to prison. I think Child Line had just been launched, but we agreed we just couldn't take the chance. No one ever believed me about anything else, so I just couldn't risk it.

In a way I still blamed my family for making me believe I was such a liar and that nothing I said would ever be taken seriously. If I had been given a little support, I might have found the strength to tell, to help prevent those people doing it again.

For what seemed like hours we sat there talking. Molly seemed almost empty and spoke about things like they were still happening. She assured me it wasn't that bad anymore and hadn't been for years, after dad took us away.

"Mum has changed," she said. She never hits Kassie, but she still beats the older ones. Molly told me of the times mum would smash her head off the wall, and how she got pregnant.

Mum had apparently thrown a party for her 14th birthday and had insisted on making her drink alcohol. Mum found it highly amusing watching her stagger around drunk. Molly said she couldn't remember much, just feeling sick and sorry for herself, but when she woke up the following morning she discovered a strange guy in her bed. She explained how she lay there knowing that mum had set her up to get drunk so she would have sex with this guy. She said she hadn't seen him since.

She had been late for her period. Mum took her to a clinic and forced her to have an abortion, bullying her as usual by saying if anyone ever found out she would be labelled a "slag" for the rest of her life.

"I'll never forgive her for that," Molly said.

"There's a lot more than that, not to forgive her for," I said. I urged her to remember, raising my eyebrows in sarcasm so she would know I was referring to the bad stuff.

It's amazing what you can get used to, I thought. *But, yes, you can get used to violence and sexual abuse.* I was about 13 when I realised that it was all so wrong. Looking at Molly I thought, *My stepmother sold our little bodies to the highest bidder. We were used as prostitutes to earn her money, whilst we posed for child pornography and stuff for Uncle Joe. How could any human being do that to a child?*

Molly told me how Uncle Joe suddenly stopped coming round, how the neighbours started standing up for them arguing with mum about how she treated her kids. They told her they would be watching and that's when Uncle Joe started staying away. But Molly still visited him sometimes, mainly to do photo stuff for other men and to earn a bit of money. Even after that he would still grope her privates or make her suck his dick. The really painful stuff stopped after I left.

Did I cause it then? I wondered. *I must have surely if it stopped after I left?* Well that's what I thought for many years, but how could a nine-year-old be responsible?

I looked over at Kassie.

"Mum never touches her," Molly said with anger and jealousy in her voice, nodding towards Kassie. "What is so special about her?"

I could hear the bitterness in her voice. I looked at Kassie wondering what was so special. She wasn't pretty. In fact she was quite unattractive. She had a large frame and tried hard to be noticed, being very loud in everything she did. I really didn't know what to say to her. After all I didn't know her. Molly was the only one who wanted to come and visit dad. The others didn't want to. Molly said they were still angry that dad had left and didn't really want anything to do with him.

Fair enough, I thought. *I wonder how much mum soured their feelings.* I didn't suppose I could blame them really. Dad had only taken me and Alex and failed to rescue them from that witch.

"How was the chocolate Yule log?" I asked and laughed at Molly. It broke the ice as she remembered when we made it at school. I told her I was gutted I had to leave it with her and not tasting it has scarred me for life. We both laughed out loud. Mum wouldn't let us take enough ingredients for two so we had to share and make one together.

"It was very nice what we got to have of it," she chuckled.

Molly seemed distant. It was almost like she had a mental impairment. I had to drag a conversation out of her. She was a closed book. I was sad when I had to go because I knew there was no one to protect her. She was so weak and vulnerable and I knew I couldn't be there for her. We promised we would be back together one day, maybe share a flat or something, anything, to get her away from mum.

Chapter 19

The weekend was getting close and I had arranged to meet Dave in Leicester. I was nervously excited as I stuffed a bag full of my favourite gear, my best shoes and not forgetting of course, my makeup bag. I was going to hide it somewhere nearby so that when Friday arrived, no one at the children's home would find out that I was missing until it was too late. I had a few quid saved and knew it would be plenty to get me to Leicester, bearing in mind trains were usually free for me. All I needed was enough to get me to Dave. I thought, *Maybe I ought to pay this time as I can't risk getting caught.* If I could get myself there, Dave would sort out the rest.

The bag I had stuffed under the front hedge of the neighbouring house was damp and as I grabbed it out, I prayed that my clothes would be okay. It was very early in the morning. The birds hadn't been up long and were full of song. It was just starting to get light too. I had to get a shift on, the day staff would be in soon to take over from the nights. Then they would start their normal rounds waking everyone up, preparing breakfast and pushing and annoying the kids to get ready. No one wanted to go to school and no one made it easy for the staff. I had to hurry.

The Milkman was passing in his milk float as I walked up the road. He looked at me funnily as if to say, *What on Earth are you doing out at this ungodly time of the morning?* I hurried on up the road sticking close to the fences. It was freezing cold, but then it was only early spring.

As I got to the main road I immediately started hitchhiking. I had to get a ride before staff passed by and spotted me. I knew it wouldn't take me long to get a lift though, it never did. *A young girl with huge boobs in a miniskirt?* It was just a matter of minutes. The guy who picked me up gave me a lecture on how I was too young to hitchhike and shouldn't take rides from strangers.

Blah fuckin' blah fuckin' blah! I only had to listen to him for about 15 minutes and then we would be at the town where I could get the train. He said he was an accountant and proceeded to lecture me on getting a good education. Of course, I agreed with everything he said. I just nodded and gazed out the window planning what Dave and I were going to do with the rest of our lives.

I had to waste the day doing not much really. My train wasn't until late that evening, so I made my way to some friends. I spent the day watching TV and wandering around town or sitting in a café watching the world go by.

It was Friday night and a lot of people would be on their way out clubbing or going home for the weekend from work. I had just enough money for my ticket and held on to it tightly, picking at the corners of it as I sat in the waiting room for the train. I had to buy a ticket for once. It had taken so much planning to get it all right, I couldn't afford to risk getting caught on this night of all nights. It nearly killed me handing over my money when I knew I could have bunked the trip. The risk just wasn't worth it.

The waiting room was old and musty. It needed a good lick of paint and some new seats. The old wooden benches were covered in scratched graffiti. I was over an hour early so I spent the time people watching and reading graffiti. It wasn't the first time I had run away but this was different. It was the first time I really meant it and knew I wasn't going back. I didn't ever want to go back. Usually I was just going for a weekend to a rally or a gig, but this time I was going for life.

I still hadn't seen dad or Maggie. I think they had moved on and forgot about me. I heard they had been to Italy with Alex. *Nice one,* I thought a little jealous that, as usual, I missed out. I was difficult. I knew I was and I really don't think things would have been any different if Maggie had loved me. I knew that I wasn't wanted and if I was going to make anything out of my life it was going to be up to me. It was time to get on with it.

I sat in the waiting room that day doing a lot of dreaming of what my future life would be. *What sort of house will Dave and I live in? Will we have kids? What will we do for money?*

Dave was in the army but hated it. He hated not being able to do what he wanted when he wanted. He was pushed into the army because his brother was in already and his dad had an army career. So it was expected of Dave too. The only thing he liked about it was the rugby, and I had to admit that he was pretty good. I think he was just as much a rebel at heart as I was really, but I know he used to feed off of my attitude. It excited him and gave him courage, he often told me.

Waiting for the train I wondered, *Will I be missed by anyone, ever? I don't think school will miss me. School is rubbish anyway.* I only got on with my year head. She seemed to understand me but then I did spend a lot of the time I was at school in her office. My other teachers had washed their hands of me. I did the work when I felt like it or if I understood it. I wouldn't be bothered if it was difficult. I would just walk out. Being honest it was easier if I didn't understand the work. I was far too proud and too cool to ask for help.

I would also get sent directly to the year head's office if I chose not to wear school uniform. My trademark miniskirts or ski-pants were often what I chose to wear. I told the kids home not to bother when they bought me a new school uniform. I wouldn't wear it anyway so why not just give me the money instead? I could then spend it in charity shops on original sixties clothing. But of course they insisted I try to conform by wearing school uniform. *Who are they kidding?* I refused to put it on and said if they wanted me to go to school then, "I will wear what I like, or not go at all. I have street cred to think about, you know?"

I hardly went to school anyway playing truant for days, sometimes weeks at a time. It was hardly surprising that I wasn't doing very well academically. I was always popular, probably because of my rebellious ways. Other kids found it highly hilarious if I mouthed off at one of my teachers or walked out of class to go and have a ciggie behind the toilet blocks. Nothing ever happened when I got caught. Maybe worse case scenario I'd get sent to the year head who would greet me with a sigh, "Okay Abbie, what have you done this time?"

I have to admit, actually she was really cool, that year head. She was pretty much the only nice thing I remembered about my school days. She wasn't a pretty lady, quite broad and not feminine. She had her hair cut short and never wore much makeup apart from a bit of lippy. She empathized with my plight, not like the rest of the teachers who hated me. They couldn't be bothered. In fact, the whole school stopped bothering when I went into care.

The loudspeakers rang out and I jumped out of my daydreaming. "Train to Leicester will be arriving at platform two in five minutes." It sounded like someone was pinching their nose and talking as close to the microphone as possible. *This is it,* I thought, *the moment I've been waiting for, my ticket to paradise.* I took a deep breath, collected my bag and wandered onto the platform. Whilst standing with everyone else I had a sense of fear as the butterflies started fluttering in my tummy and built up to a full blown fight or flight adrenaline rush.

Hurry up train! I tapped my foot with impatience and looked around the crowd nervously. *What if I'm found before the train leaves?* I edged my way forward through the mob to the white line on the platform. I don't remember being this nervous before, not for anything really. The fact that I had paid for my ticket should have reassured me. *What if something goes wrong? I could be stuck in that kid's home until I'm 18.*

Chapter 20

The train pulled into the station at last. I boarded the nearest steps pushing my way through the carriages until I found a spare seat. I put my stuff on the overhead shelf and sat down, still nervous. I looked around and out of the window, checking to be sure there was no one I knew from the children's home. There were some girls in the seats immediately in front of me, all giggly, apparently out on a hen night. They were all dressed new wave, Gary Numan or Ultravox style. To my left was an elderly gentleman with a young girl who looked like his daughter and in front of him were two lads. They appeared to be army boys as they had no hair, just short back and side haircuts, a total giveaway really. They made eye contact and then turned to each other whispering. They started giggling acting like kids. I must have been in a great mood, so excited about meeting Dave. Any other time I would've given them a mouthful just for looking at me. I had beaten up girls for less, and they wouldn't be the first guys I had smacked down a peg or two.

The motion of the train sent me off into another daydream. I stared out of the window, now at the night sky, looking at lights in the distance, house lights and street lights all being left behind. Feeling the motion of the train, the budum budum budum on the tracks was enough to send anyone to sleep. I pictured Dave being at the station waiting for me and taking me round to his friend's house. We had planned to be staying there for a few days until we got a place sorted.

It felt like an eternity on the train, although it probably was just about two hours in reality. I had to change trains in London and was then on a further train for another two hours. My hands felt all clammy as the train approached the station in Leicester. I checked that I had my purse and all my belongings and then made my way to the partition section by the door. I was so excited, I wanted to be the first off of the train. I needed to see my Dave.

I walked through the station, following the crowd of people towards the exit just like a sheep. The station was massive. I began to worry I would never find him there. I took some solace though from knowing that no one from the home would find me. I made my way to the station entrance, the collection and drop off point. He was more likely to be there than anywhere I figured. I looked around but Dave was nowhere to be seen. I paced up and down staring at stranger's faces. *Do I know any of them? Had he sent a friend to collect me?* I watched people greet loved ones and get into taxi's and cars, one after another pulling up to where I stood. The station was a beehive of activity. As time went on the station got quieter and quieter and still no Dave. *I wonder what happened? He better have a bloody good excuse.*

I searched through my bags to find his friend's telephone number. I had kept it from ages ago. Dave used to stay there and I had rung him from the children's home telephone on several occasions. I walked over to the red pillar box telephone and dialled the number. It rang and rang forever before I hung up, and then I started to worry. *Maybe he's on his way? Maybe he got stuck in traffic? Who knows?* I had all sorts of reasons running through my tiny mind. I stayed at the station for two more hours before I gave up and started making my way into the town centre. I remembered Dave saying his mate lived in the town centre in an apartment over some shops, so hopefully, I would find them.

The walk took me about 45 minutes and my feet were killing me. I had blisters on my heels and my toes felt like they were in a vice. Winkle picker shoes were not the best or most comfortable for hiking, but then again, *I didn't plan to do all this walking, did I?*

I found the town centre and wandered up and down the high street. The night clubs had kicked out. It was about 2:30am and I was freezing cold and hungry. I had all of £1.80 in my pocket, just enough to buy a one-way ticket so I couldn't even get back on the train. The security was tight on the way up, no way I would get away with hiding on the train. I attempted to ring the friend's flat about 20 times more, every time I passed a telephone box I rang and there was still no answer. I looked around for somewhere warmer, apart from shop doorways there was nothing. So I gave the phone number one last try before going out of town to find somewhere to sleep. *At last! I can't believe it.* Someone picked up.

It sounded like Andy, "Hello?"

"Where the fuck have you been?" I bellowed down the phone.

"Out at a gig," he replied. "Abbie is that you?" in a guilty tone.

"Where's Dave?" I enquired with warning in my voice. I sensed something wrong, the pause was far too long before I got a reply. He was about to say something when I heard giggling in the background.

"Abbie? Abbie is that you?"

"I'm in Leicester Andy! For fuck sake where the hell is Dave?" I was frustrated. The giggling became louder but the beeps went off and I was forced to put more money in. I was rapidly running out of change.

"Where is he?" I shouted. I knew in my heart of hearts where he was. The girls in the background were not alone. I thought I had heard Dave's voice amongst the giggling.

"Tell him I am here will you?" I pleaded. I was deflated and scared. *Why is he doing this to me? We spoke just the other day, and he knew I was coming to Leicester.*

"Tell him I will wait in the town centre, Andy."

"Okay." He hung up.

It was clear he was uncomfortable, but his saying, "okay," confirmed that Dave WAS at Andy's flat. Not only that, he had to know I was on the phone. Andy had said my name several times, so what was he playing at? I couldn't do anything now, I was stuck. I couldn't go anywhere just in case he came to look for me. I had told Andy where in the town I was going to wait. So I found a seat and parked myself there and waited, and waited and waited, fumes coming off my head.

Time ticked on. It was 4:30 in the morning and still no sign of Dave. I had not slept and was wondering how long it would be before the birds began singing again? I lay down on the seat and huddled up into a ball. My coat was useless and wasn't keeping me warm at all. I lay there shivering at times, wishing the morning would come so I could go and find Dave. I had no idea what he was doing, but I had to find out why he hadn't met me at the station. *What happened to our plans? What was I going to do now?* I heard footsteps and bolted upright relieved. I turned around with a smile expecting to see Dave. Two police officers stood there staring at me.

"Shit! Shit!" I said under my breath. *Now what? If I run for it they'll give chase. I don't stand a chance. They'd catch me for sure running in these bloody shoes.*

One of them said, "Hello little lady what are you doing out here?"

I explained, "I was supposed to meet a friend but he didn't arrive at the train station. I telephoned him and he should be here soon. I must stay here or he won't find me."

"Sorry, we can't do that. If we leave you here anything could happen."

I spent the next half an hour trying to persuade them in a nice way and then in not so nice a way to "leave me alone and go and arrest some real criminals."

They wouldn't have any of it though and said I didn't look old enough to be out at night on my own.

"Unless you tell us who you are and where you live, we will have to take you to the Police station for your own safety."

I knew at that point I had lost. I broke down then, hung my head and sighed.

Just once, I thought, whimpering to myself. *Just once in my life, I'd like something to go right. Maybe I can find Dave tomorrow.*

Chapter 21

The Police car was warm. I was actually pleased to have some heat. I had been outside pretty much since 4:00 am the previous day and I was chilled to the bone. I hadn't slept apart from a cat nap on the train and I was starving hungry. I told myself that if I had planned it better, I would have taken some more money or at least made some sandwiches.

The desk sergeant at the Police station was insistent I give a name, so I made one up and was taken to a cell where I could get some sleep. Cells didn't scare me, I settled in and dozed off quickly. I must have only had about three hours sleep when I was woken up by the smell of toast. A policewoman came waltzing into the cell.

"Morning lovely," she said. She was a bit cheerful for so early in the morning, but I wasn't going to turn down the chance of a cup of tea and toast by being rude.

The sound of people walking up and down the corridors of the Police station let me know it was getting busier. I felt like a right criminal put in the cells, but for the fact that on this one occasion I hadn't done anything wrong, *In my opinion*.

After awhile the policewoman came back and asked me to go with her to an interview room. I followed her through a few doors, down a corridor and into a side room. When we walked in, there was an older lady waiting. She smiled at me as I entered and sat myself down at the table. After a few minutes of her explaining that she was the "on call" social worker from the local social services department, she said she was going to have to find me somewhere to stay. If I didn't own up to who I was and whom I was supposed to meet, she had no choice.

I can't tell them the truth, they'll send me to the home! I would get Dave into big trouble if I told them he was up here too, so I sat in silence whilst they waffled on to me about being sent back to my cell to think about things. As the cell door clunked shut I knew deep down it was over. The social worker told me that I would be going to a Leicestershire children's home until I decided to tell the truth.

I sat there reasoning that even if I stayed quiet in Leicester, Dave had brought this on himself. He hadn't met me, he had left me to roast and he obviously didn't want the things that I did or the things we planned together. *The big fat liar.* I could sense that on the telephone with girls giggling and having fun in the background. He didn't need me so what was the point in my staying loyal or staying around?

I was feeling depressed as I finally admitted to lying and told the police officer my real name. They found me on the computer system. The children's home had reported me as missing. All that was needed now was to arrange for them to take me back home. *Home? Is that what it is? It might be a children's home but it certainly isn't home to me.*

The police drove me all the way back. They were actually quite nice. Listening to the radio and stopping for lunch on the way, they looked on it as a day out. It did take several hours.

I didn't know what to expect on my return. *Am I in trouble? What will happen now?* The police gave me lectures about behaving myself and to stop wasting everyone's time. *Yes that's it, at the end of the day, I'm just a waste of time.* Even Dave couldn't be bothered with me anymore. My family couldn't be bothered so why should I? I planned that I would just end it all. I would kill myself and have it over and done with, then I wouldn't be a burden.

The staff were surprisingly welcoming when we arrived back home. I had thought after all the agro I had caused everyone, I was in for a lecture or two. But I was pleasantly surprised when I was told to go and have a bath and they would sort out some dinner for me.

The other kids ran up to me on the stairs, all excited to hear the stories of my adventure. I had nothing to say. I certainly didn't want to tell the other kids that my boyfriend had left me to make a complete fool of myself and how I was left stranded in a strange city, sleeping on a bench. *Err, no, I think I'll keep this adventure to myself.*

I had nothing to say to anyone; the staff all tried talking to me. They were aware of what had happened, the police had told them. They gave me space for the night and I ate dinner and went to bed. I didn't have any arguments left. All I wanted to do was sleep. Hopefully, tomorrow Dave would ring me saying how sorry he was and how it was all a big mistake, that it wasn't him at Andy's flat and that it must have been someone else's voice. But my heart knew the truth, and I knew that even if he did call, I had nothing to say.

The phone did ring the next day but it was my social worker Albert. The children's home had told him that I was not welcome there anymore. He was told he had to find an alternative placement for me. I was a bad influence on the other kids and causing unrest in the home.

"Why did you fucking bring me back, if you're getting rid of me?" I screamed at them as I stomped up the stairs. I was furious. I could have stayed up in Leicester and met Dave. *What if Dave had turned up five minutes after I was found by the police? And they had the audacity to say, "You're back now so you can fuck off!"* Well, that's what it felt like to me. I ran up the rest of the stairs to be on my own, slammed my door and threw myself down on my bed and buried my head in my pillow. I was angry, upset, rejected, all of the above, but no tears would come. I couldn't remember the last time I had cried real tears. I screamed anger into my pillow.

I wasn't interested in dinner when I was called down later. All I wanted was to be left alone. People only came into my life to hurt me or wreck it, to wreck my plans and spoil any fun I might have. *What is the point in doing anything to make my life happier when so called well meaning adults are there to mess it up?*

Chapter 22

I lay on my bed in the children's home staring at one of the pictures and deep in thought when suddenly I heard voices. I recognised the unmistakeable Welsh accent. Someone was on the way up the stairs because I was usually unable to hear more than about a flight and a half down from my room. I remained on my bed unconcerned. I had a cloud over me. I really couldn't be bothered with anything or anyone. A gentle knock at my door brought me back out of my self-pitying daydream of how I was going to end it all. I ignored the knock, rolled over in bed and turned my back to the door. It got louder.

"Hello hun, it's Albert, can I come in?"

"Do what you like, you're going to anyway," I hurled at him through the old wooden door. The door creaked open and he entered gingerly and perched himself on the white wicker chair in my room.

"You've gone and done it this time Lassie, no more chances!" He gazed at me with a stern face expecting some sort of reply, or maybe an explosion.

Is he asking me or stating a fact? I wondered. "Fuck off."

"Why Abbie? Why are you so hell bent on hurting yourself. No one else is getting hurt apart from you?"

With a quick glance at his face it looked like he genuinely cared. But I turned away. I just gazed out the window at the sky trying to put him to the back of my mind. He was a nice bloke and I didn't want to lose my temper. He seemed to be on my side. Every time he came he left me with fags or cash to buy fags. He always made sure I had money for clothes and he was easy to squeeze for extra coin. He was probably the only person left I could wrap around my finger. I had a bit of a soft spot for him. "Cupboard love," the staff said behind his back.

"Where now then?" I mumbled still staring at the window. He stood up and started walking back to the door.

"I've got a suitcase in my car for you. I'll fetch it lass and we'll get you packed. You'll find out soon enough," he said on his way out the door without looking back.

I took my time in packing my belongings. I certainly wasn't about to rush for anyone. I checked my makeup, hair and put on my favourite black ski pants. I made my way down the stairs to get some food. It was a hive of activity as I walked down the hall into the dining room. But as I entered it fell totally silent. I mean it was deathly quiet. No one would even look at me. It was like they felt some sort of guilt or remorse and didn't know what to say. I really didn't care though, grabbing some bread and shoving a couple of slices of bacon in between. I walked outside and into the garden wondering, *The way they look I must be going to the gallows.*

All of a sudden I snapped and my brain went out of gear. I was at boiling point, pacing up and down clenching my fists. I wanted to explode. I wanted to scream but I didn't know why. I threw my bacon butty across the garden and lit a cigarette.

"Come on hun," Albert called after me. "Let's get this over with and get on our way."

We went back to my room, squeezed the rest of my stuff into the one suitcase and walked out to his car. He stood there at the door talking with staff and signing a piece of paper.

He turned and waved at the other kids and called out, "Cheerio." They were looking out of their windows. I didn't look at them. I looked away into the trees as we drove out of the gravel driveway. The gardener caught my eye as we drove past and gave me a wink, a smile and a nod and walked away to his shed. *Hmmm,* I thought, *that's exactly where he was the first time I arrived at this godforsaken place.*

The drive to Margate didn't take long. I was in a daze for most of the journey, planning to run away at the first chance I got. *But where?*

"Not long now," Albert said. "No other home will take you dearie. You used up all your nine lives. Now you're on your own."

"On my own?" I said back to him. I was shocked and my voice went all high pitched, "I'm not even 16 yet, how can I be on my own?" I laughed nervously.

"You're far too difficult, Abbie. You're too old to be fostered, and the children's homes don't want you. So the next thing is 'supported lodgings.'"

"Supported lodgings?" I did my parrot impression again.

As we drove along the seafront, I got pretty excited about suddenly being in control of my own life. *Am I going to live near the sea?* I hoped so. *The sea means freedom. Its power is eternal, I love the sea.* Maybe my love of the sea came from my dad. He was a merchant seaman in his younger days so maybe it was in my blood. *One day I'll go to sea and maybe work on the ships.* But then I thought, *Maybe not.* As much as I loved the sea, I had a more than a healthy respect for it. I wouldn't even swim in it. The strength of the waves and the current and the thought of sharks scared me.

We pulled up outside a large terraced house. It had four floors and each window at the front had a balcony. I was pretty excited, *Wow! This could be good, especially if I get a room facing the sea.* The row of houses on the seafront all looked the same.

They looked like something off a postcard, all perfect and all staring out over the ocean.

As we got out of the car a sharp sea breeze hit me. The smell of fish and the noise of people on the beach, kids running around having fun, I found it all captivating. It was half-term at school and the beach was busy. I felt like I was arriving on holiday. *This is brilliant*, I thought to myself. *It certainly doesn't feel like a punishment. Is it meant to feel like one? Will they be giving me a taste of the good life then snatching it away? What is "supported lodgings" anyway?*

We made our way up the steep front steps then walked around the path to the side of the building and to the side door. A tall, blonde woman answered the door bell. She had a baby resting on her hip. It was busy grabbing her hair and trying to stuff it in its mouth alongside the dummy that was already getting sucked the life out of. The baby looked at me and made a few noises. It gave me a big smile and dropped its dummy onto the pavement to reveal a mouth with no teeth and a little gummy smile.

Sweet kid, I thought and smiled back.

"My name is Evie and this is my home," she said bending down to pick up the dummy. She walked back inside beckoning us to follow. The ceiling seemed to go up forever, it was so high. The carpet was red and fluffy and the sort you could sink your toes into. It brought back memories of my real mum sitting on the landing.

She walked into the kitchen and pointed towards the big wooden table.

"Have a seat," she said as she walked over the other side of the room and put the baby into a playpen. It immediately started banging toys and making lots of noise. Evie looked tired and gave a huge sigh as she put the kettle on.

"I expect people here to have respect for one another," obviously aimed at me.

"Are you talking to me?" I enquired.

"There's a list of house rules that everyone is expected to follow. If you don't follow them then you're out, no second chances I'm afraid." She looked at me and handed me a sheet of paper.

I shrugged my shoulders and did my very best to keep my mouth shut. I could see Albert cringing, probably hoping I didn't blow it before I had even seen my room. She shouted for a guy to come and watch the baby while she showed me around. She led the way around a maze of stairways and corridors.

This place is like the tardis from Dr Who, I thought. It was huge inside, a lot bigger than it appeared from the outside. Two floors up and around several corridors was my room. She opened the door and stood aside so I could go in. It was very basic and small in comparison to my last room. It had a single bed, a dark wood single wardrobe with built in drawers and a small matching dressing table with a table top fridge.

"You get four slices of bread and one pint of milk a day," she said. "That way if you blow your money you won't starve." She smiled at me. The best thing about the room was that it was at the front of the property. I had a small balcony, not big enough to go out onto really but I had a full view of the sea from my room. *Wow,* I thought, *what a view!*

"Well?" she asked.

"I am very happy with it," I replied.

"Good, good, then let's move on and see the rest." She walked out of the room and led the way around the house showing me a shared bathroom, the toilet and then a shared communal kitchen and lounge.

"There are eight people living here," she said to Albert. "Abbie will be the youngest. Elvin is the eldest at 18, but he's moving out in a few months." She waffled on about rules and respecting privacy and the like and handed me the key to my room together with the key to the front door. I was to use the front door only as the side entrance was hers. "I've got work to do," she said. "I'll let the two of you settle."

Albert handed me £80.

"This is to tide you over until you start getting your dole money. Don't blow it, it's for food." He arranged that he would come by once a month to check on me then walked out of the door,

"But when. .?" I called after him.

He turned to give me some explanation.

"You wanted your independence Hun," he said sarcastically whilst grinning, "Well, now you've got it, let's see what you do. Don't BLOW IT!"

I think it was the most authoritative thing he ever said to me. It almost made me giggle. *Albert couldn't argue his way out of a paper bag,* I thought, *never mind get all tough now!*

"I will see you in a few weeks," he called up to me as I waved to him from my balcony.

Chapter 23

I'd heard of dole money, but I didn't really know what it was or how it worked. I'd figure that out when I had to. But one thing was sure, I felt rich with £80 in my pocket to do with whatever I wanted. I can honestly say it was the most money I had ever held in one go that had been given to me honestly and not stolen. Evie said she would take me to the supermarket and show me around the place tomorrow, but for tonight it would have to be fish and chips.

I wandered up the seafront, taking in all the sights and sounds. It was getting dark but the lights from the arcades lit up the night sky making it a Technicolor evening. The sound of fruit machines and music from cafés filled the air. It was a magical moment and I could hardly believe my good fortune. *To hell with the children's home, this is living.*

It didn't take me long to spot the scooters parked outside one of the arcades. It was Margate after all. Nervously, I walked up to the arcade peeking in the window as I neared to see if I knew anyone in there. I recognised no one but just as I reached the end of the arcade, I noticed a couple of scooterists playing pinball. There was a girl sitting on the edge of the car racing game. I could tell she was not impressed with what the boys were playing. She was more interested in her shoes, pointing and putting her foot in different directions.

Maybe they're new, I thought. I don't know where the bravery came from but I walked into the arcade, past the noise of the arms being pulled on fruit machines and people playing *Space Invaders*. I walked straight up to the girl, smiled and said, "Hi, I've just moved here. Is there anywhere to go in Margate in the evening."

She looked me up and down and then smiled back. "Yeah sure, hang with us a while and we'll show you around."

That was the first time I met Lilly. I think she was pleased there was another girl on the scene. I spent the evening with them hanging out on the seafront and making arrangements to meet up the following day. I made my way back to my new digs relieved. At least now I knew someone in Margate. I had found a fellow mod friend here, someone who I sensed was going to become a close friend as we'd hit it off straight away.

Outside my room was the promised bread, wrapped in cling film and beside it was a small carton of milk. I carried it into my room and put it into the fridge. The fridge looked pretty stark with just milk in it.

I unpacked my things and sat on the end of the bed listening to the sounds of my new environs. I didn't have a TV or a radio so I just sat there for what seemed an eternity. I could hear the traffic on the seafront, people giggling and walking by eating their candy floss. I stood up and went over to the window. Leaning on the wall I looked out and watched. I could see the multi-coloured sky from the arcade lights and people walking up and down the beach. I couldn't believe how busy it was at night. *How will I sleep through this noise?* I thought to myself. So I went for another look around the house and found the shared kitchen. There were a few guys in the sitting room. All got up to come and say hello. I was a bit shocked by their friendliness. They must have thought I was stuck up or something, as I didn't really have much to say. I made a hasty retreat to my room.

I threw myself onto my bed and just lay there listening to the sound of traffic. *Is this my new life? Am I here forever?* I wondered what Dave was doing? What about Alex, Dad and Maggie? Not that I cared really. They obviously didn't care about me or I wouldn't be here. I wondered if Albert would tell them where I was. My mind wouldn't stop working. It was going round and round thinking about my life and how I really didn't have anyone I could trust anymore, apart from Albert. I didn't even have any pills to help me sleep. That was something I needed to work on the following day. I made a mental note. *Drugs.*

Albert rang saying that Dave had been trying to get in touch and left his address for me. I took the opportunity to write a letter, telling him that I felt it really wouldn't work anymore. Because of what he had done, I felt lied to and cheated on, that he had deserted me in Leicester and how it had made me feel inside. I told him I was on my own now with my own place. I had no one and it was best left that way. I didn't want to drag him down with me. I told him how I was bad news for him and that he should just move on. I guess I sounded pretty heartless. I didn't have anything nice to say, not after what he did to me, leaving me to the police.

I wasn't really on my own in the house, I still had to abide by the rules. *In my world there aren't any rules!* I wasn't allowed boys in my room, for example. I still had someone telling me what I could and couldn't do, so although I had my own place, I really wasn't on my own where I could make ALL the decisions. There weren't any rules about times to be in. I could stay out all night if I wanted to, but I had to check in on a daily basis and sign the day book, so Evie could check that I was still alive.

Evie took me around the neighbourhood. She showed me the supermarket and the unemployment office. She suggested

I continue with my education, at least until my exams which were scheduled for the following summer.

"Albert has arranged for you to go to your old school, just to do the exams. So it's up to you if you want some help with home schooling."

"I don't need any help," I said. "I'll be fine." *What is she thinking? I can't be bothered doing exams. What's all the fuss over education anyway?*

My fridge looked good. I stocked it with various yoghurts, packets of cooked meat, cheese, and I had some fresh juice and chicken for tonight's tea. I had no idea how to cook really, but I guessed I was about to learn pretty sharpish. I set aside a drawer in the wardrobe where I kept packets of crisps and biscuits. I put up a few posters of *Paul Weller and the Jam*, as well as pictures of *The Who* and the *Beatles*. I had purchased them from a shop along the promenade. My room seemed a little more like home.

I met Lilly that night down on the seafront. There were several scooters there, all wanting to meet the new girl in town. It didn't take long before I was a part of the group spending most of my time with them. I went to parties, to gigs and on all the scooter rallies and weekenders I could get a lift to. Evie didn't mind the weekenders as long as I told her I was going and when I would be back. I couldn't do enough partying. Most of my friends who lived at home required their parent's permission, so a lot of the time I was able to go to gigs when my friends weren't. It sort of defeated the benefit of my having all this freedom. *No one else does, so what's the point?*

I spent most of the dole on going out, snacks, cigarettes and drugs when I could get them. I lived pretty much on beans on toast. Whomever I was hanging around depended what drugs I used. I tried glue-sniffing with some of my skinhead friends the year before, but I hated that. I couldn't understand what the draw was. It made me sick and totally out of control. On top of that, the shop keepers got wise to it and started asking for

ID. Other times I would take pills, never knowing what they were or what they did to you. I wasn't really bothered either as long as they gave me a buzz and an escape.

Lilly and I became inseparable. She lived at home with her parents and younger sister and was always in trouble too. When I looked back, I probably caused most of it, pushing her to do things she wouldn't have done without me around. We became like sisters, swapping clothes and borrowing each other's things. She was extremely kind to everyone, totally different to how I was, but that was why we got on so well. She was so easily manipulated.

Lilly was very pretty too. She had short blonde hair which she backcombed, her makeup the same as my trademark, bitch lines and white or pink lipstick. We would quite literally spend hours trailing around the second-hand shops searching for authentic 60's clothing. There were some fantastic bargains to be had, and we always looked good. Walking down the road together we projected an air of, *Don't even bother, we're too good for you.* We strutted with an attitude, but it didn't stop the guys looking or trying to go out with us. We were never short of boyfriends, and it was nice to be able to choose.

Chapter 24

By the time the band came on stage the crowd packed in, a mass of throbbing hormones. Although not as manic as some mod gigs there was still a vibrant and explosive atmosphere. Electric guitar magic was in the air and amps were cranked to the max. We all surged towards the stage as the first song, *Now It's Gone*, echoed through the hall. I was psyched! This was what I lived for, that nerve tingle of mass hysteria. All four members of the band looked amazingly cool. The energy and pent up excitement of the crowd built to a crescendo as *The Chords* rattled through one mod anthem after another. It was like a nuclear bomb ready to explode. I looked around recognising several faces in the crowd. The north London mod's were there in high numbers. They normally didn't turn up with quite so big a group, but they were there alongside other groups that I had never seen, but all great just the same. Mod scenes were popping up all over Britain.

The mod revival craze is here, I thought, *and I'm right in the middle of it!*

Some of the Shepherds Bush boys were there too, more familiar faces I'd seen around, but I wasn't convinced we could rely on them in a fight. They were a bit unpredictable in a ruck. Normally we mods were solid together, but a conflict of interest stirred the crowd: some wanted to party and some wanted a scrap. I thought, *Only Kev from the Canterbury mob is one-hundred-percent trustworthy.* You could always rely on him in a brawl.

There were a few of the Peckham lads present whom I exchanged nods with, but our mates, Pete and his mob, weren't there. *Probably still recovering from Saturday,* I smiled to myself remembering the mayhem at the London train station after the gig last week. A few of the lads and I had tried phoning Pete since, but funnily enough, he never seemed to be in. It was like he just disappeared. We counted him out! The band's set was coming to an end. The closing song, *Maybe Tomorrow*, built up the atmosphere signalling the end of another immense performance. In my view, *The Chords* was one of the best mod bands, outside *The Jam,* on the circuit.

Liquor, sweat and other body-fluids dripped from everywhere, teenagers, walls and the ceiling, and, finally, the band left the stage. Adrenaline pumped through the crowd in anticipation of what would happen outside adding a certain something to the violent atmosphere the band helped fuel. I grabbed Lilly by the hand and pulled her through towards where some of my friends, Harry, Kev and their mates were gathering. Harry nodded over at me, winked, and turned to his mob.

"Everyone ready then?" he screamed.

They knew what he meant and his challenge was met with a few nods and murmurs. No one was in the mood for talking, they were all too busy hyping themselves up to be tougher than the rest.

"Okay!" he yelled.

The way he conducted the orchestra of teenagers excited me even more. *Harry is sooo damn cool!*

"Lets fuckin' get it over with. Go!" Kev shouted as he began moving towards the entrance, pushing the crowd to the front door. I had seen what masses of wild young lads could do and my stomach was turning somersaults. My mouth was dry and my heart pounded as I walked or rather, was carried along by the crowd. A battalion of bodies surged against me from behind and pushed me into the cool, night air. To be honest, at that very moment, I felt like I was going to be sick. I was light headed and my legs felt like jelly. Lilly squeezed my hand in a death grip trying to hang on. I turned and smiled at her pretending I was cool with it all. The truth be told, I was scared shitless, but I thrived on it. Lilly looked petrified as we headed along the side of the bridge towards the station. It was only a matter of a few minutes away, but it felt more like miles. We were blocked with railway arches on one side and a high brick wall of the housing estates on the other. It was the perfect place for an ambush, and I smelled trouble! There were about 60 of us who had left together for the train. The rest remained behind for the usual disco and to have a few drinks. Most of us had to leave in order to get the last tube home or some of our mates would be in serious shit with their parents. We made it all the way to the junction in the road near the station when I heard a rumble like an approaching thunderstorm. *It's a relief really, and about time too,* I thought, knowing what to expect. All the waiting had been doing my head in. Once it started and really kicked off, you didn't have time to think or worry, you just shifted into auto-pilot. It was fight or flight, or in most cases both!

First a bottle smashed into the head of one of Kev's mates who immediately fell to the deck. It sounded like someone dropped a water-balloon and blood shot everywhere. Then came the barrage.

"Shit! Run!" Kev screamed.

I could see them in the ally by the junction charging toward us, hundreds of them it seemed, like some kind of nightmare. They were lobbing missiles of all descriptions from the estate on the other side, bits of wood, bottles, dustbins and road cones. You name it, it flew at us like a driving hailstorm. "Come on let's do it!" Harry yelled as we started to charge into them.

It was war. The same ancient instinct of tribal warfare had brought out the worst in mankind for thousands of years. This was skins versus mods, a common occurrence after gigs, mobs of drugged up kids looking for trouble.

The two groups collided in an explosive melee. I didn't know what to do? I really didn't want to let my mates down, but I had Lilly to look after and I'd promised to keep her safe. Bottles and bricks were raining down on us and, with it being so dark, it was impossible to avoid them. Silly really, but even though it was scary all the same, we couldn't stop laughing. Crash, boom, splat, blood was running in the streets and all we could do was laugh.

"We are the mods! We are the mods, we are, we are. We are the mods!" We shouted and sang in chorus. The sound of 60 people charging down the road like a herd of stampeding buffalo was unbelievable. Deafening!

Harry ran over and made up my mind for me. I'd been wondering if it was too much for Lilly. She'd never seen this kind of action before. He looked at me and screamed, "For fuck sake Abbie, get Lilly out of here! We ain't gonna be able to hold 'em off for long."

I didn't need telling again. I grabbed Lilly's hand and the two of us sprinted along the lane towards the station. I could hear a train on the tracks above us going in the same direction. *That'll do,* I thought and increased my speed. Running as fast as I could and dragging Lilly behind wasn't easy when we were both wearing winkle pickers. Even though we were out of the firing line, I felt safer somehow when I was in the middle of the mob. We were exposed, easy targets.

I could hear the rest of the mods behind me. They were all running now, running for dear life.

"Hold the tube, hold the tube. . ." they shouted.

We ran across the station car park as the train pulled in via the viaduct. Lilly and I bolted up the iron staircase into the station. It was a tight race and my 38DDs were pounding, whilst I gasped for air. I could hardly breathe.

Rudely, we shoved paying passengers to one side while we ran through the crowd like a hot knife through butter, laughing our heads off the whole time. The bystanders looked terrified as our gang of mods descended upon them. We hardly even noticed them really. They might just as well not have been there. In our haste, all our concentration was on reaching the train in time. We'd be dead at the hands of the skins if we didn't.

The doors signalled they were going to close, but we managed to get in between in time to hold them open as Lilly jumped on. I could hear shouting downstairs in the station as the mods rushed into the station and up the stairs. The guard was going mental at us for holding the doors.

"Fuck off!" I yelled. *I'm about to save lives here. Who do you think you are,, Jobsworth?*

The first of the mods were now running into the carriage as Lilly and I held the doors standing on either side. Quite a few of the lads were covered in blood, they obviously had a bad kicking. Some of them were holding wounds and groaning. I could see adrenaline-fuelled fear in their eyes. Harry and a few stragglers appeared at the top of the stairs. Harry was always one of the last to get away from the action. It was like he never wanted it to end, enjoying every waking minute.

The skinheads were right in amongst them, fists flying, Harry lashed out with a bit of metal piping. He and a couple of other lads were managing to keep the skinheads at bay as the rest of the boys jumped onto the train. One of the skins took the full force of the piping across the face, and I heard the crack of his jaw as he crumpled onto the platform in spurts of blood. His blood-curdling screams went right through me, rising above the noise of the mob.

Everyone paused for a second to give Harry enough time to jump aboard as we let go of the doors and they slammed shut with a bang. Almost immediately the train began to move away, the driver obviously aware of what was going on. A few more missiles bounced off the windows as the train sped up and out of the station. Luckily the glass held firm and we left London behind.

I gulped for air and thought, *This stuff only happens in movies. One day I'll have to write a book, but no one will believe me!* I looked around the carriage. It looked like the medical tent in the TV series, *M.A.S.H.* There were a few regular passengers on the train and they appeared terrified. Most were trying their best to move to another carriage.

I glanced across at Lilly and smiled, "What a night!"

We all started laughing together. I felt exhausted as the adrenaline bled out of my body like the air out of a leaky tire. We'd had it on their turf, their manor. Yep, we had gone down to the smoke and took the skins out. Hell yes! Yeah okay, fair enough, we got bashed a bit, but only because we were outnumbered. Our pride was intact. As calm descended over the carriage and the train continued towards Victoria, everybody started getting their breath and reflecting on the battle. Who did what and to whom? Did you see this? Did you see that? One story after another whilst we made our way home.

In my darkest days of loneliness, that's what kept me going, rallies, gigs, bank holiday weekends and street brawls. The adrenaline, the violence, the unbridled anger, the coming together of people just like me, the anarchy and the people who didn't give a toss about rules. These were my kind of people and they knew how to have a good time. They were my friends and made me feel important.

I knew it wasn't good for me, but it was all I had and all I wanted.

Chapter 25

It was almost 4:00 am by the time we got back to Harry's place. There were about ten of us who were intending to crash there. His parents were away for the weekend.

Slumping down on the sofa, I watched as the drinks were getting poured and pills shared around. We were going to watch a movie called *Clockwork Orange*. I don't honestly remember much at all because I was totally shattered. Drugs and booze took me down and I was soon out cold.

When I woke up, I was half dressed and, as usual, totally clueless as to why, or even if anything had happened. All I knew was I had tattoos that weren't there when I was compus mentus the day before. Someone must have thought it would be highly hilarious to tattoo "Mod" on the top of my arm. I had love heart tattoos on my pelvic bones, so someone had been in places they shouldn't. *I must have really been out,* I thought. *How could I get tattoos without knowing it?*

Lilly woke up in pretty much the same predicament. Someone had tattooed "CND" and "Y" on her forearm. It took her a minute to realise what had happened, then she quite literally went berserk.

"Oh my god! No! Oh my god! Who did this?" she shouted, scrubbing at her arm. It had the effect of waking the lads. They all had the look of, *What the fuck?* I could see them feeling their bruises from the night before. Lilly's tantrum was not particularly welcome on top of throbbing hangovers.

"You lot are fucking wankers!" I snarled at Kev. We had been starting to have a bit of a fling but this blew his chances as far as I was concerned.

"I didn't do anything," he pleaded grabbing for me as I stormed into the kitchen looking for my bag.

"Just fuck off and leave me alone!" I shrugged him off. I didn't want him anywhere near me.

Lilly and I grabbed our stuff and walked out of the house, followed by jeers from the lads about nice tits and ass. Kev was pleading with them to give it a break, but the boys were still far too high on drugs to listen. We stopped by the tattoo shop on the seafront but they were closed. It must have been far too early. We noted the opening times and arranged to go back to see if they could get rid of the tattoos before Lilly's parents noticed.

Lilly came back to my digs and we sat in my room trying to think of what she could say to her parents if they saw her arm. She was terrified of their reaction.

"Just wear long sleeve tops until we can get it sorted," I counselled. I couldn't think of anything clever to say. She started getting herself into a right state thinking what else might have happened.

"What if they raped us?" she said.

"What if they did?" I was very blasé about it really. "There's nothing we can do about it if they did."

"We could report it to the police," she said in between sobs.

"Sure. And what will they do clever clogs? Apart from discover we took drugs and tell your parents that is! Tell you what? You do what you like. As far as I'm concerned it's forgotten. It's not like it was planned. It was just a bunch of stoned and drugged up teenagers doing whatever. For all you know we asked them to."

"Oh fuck, I hope we're not pregnant," was all she could say.

"Me too." *Yikes! I hadn't even considered that!*

The guy in the tattoo shop said we would have to wait for them to heal and then we could get them tattooed over the top. "I can't do anything else, no one can."

"Brilliant! Just brilliant!" Lilly threw her hands up in the air exasperated as she stormed out of the shop.

"Calm down," I said.

"Now what? Long sleeves forever?"

"Just get it over with," I said. "Tell your parents now before all the scooter rallies start. That way if you get grounded, you'll be off grounding when you need to be." I was trying to make her feel better, but I don't think it worked really.

She was grounded for a month.

I hated it. Lilly and I did everything together and it felt like one of my arms was missing. I had purposely avoided the lads since that night. As far as I was concerned there wasn't anything I could do about what they had done. But I knew I couldn't trust them not to do the same again. We needed new friends and quick. Otherwise we wouldn't be able to get to the rallies and gigs without transport.

I rang around a few friends and started going out with a different gang of mods from Canterbury. They all knew me anyway, so it wasn't hard to be accepted as one of them. There weren't many girls in their crew either, so it was pretty novel for them to have a girl around. "J" was sort of the leader of that gang. He decided when and where and he became my next boyfriend. His scooter was pretty flashy. He had the *Clockwork Orange* spray painted on the side panels. It looked very tasty, and I loved riding pillion because everyone cooed over the paint job.

The lads from Margate kept pestering me all the time though. Kev kept calling round for me, or sitting outside my window on his scooter beeping and trying to get me to go out. But I couldn't be bothered with any of them anymore.

A knock on my door brought me back to reality. Evie came in and sat down.

"I thought I had better check that you're alive. Haven't seen you for ages."

"Oh? I'm okay."

She went on to tell me that Albert had visited on a few occasions but I was never in. He left his number and said if I needed anything to call. I never saw Albert again. To be honest I wondered what happened. He dropped me off four months ago and I hadn't seen him once. *So much for caring!* I thought. Just another person to come in and go out of my life. He was so sweet, I thought he was different. But I realised it was just his job to care, and I was no more than paperwork.

I looked in my mini fridge and saw a few cartons of milk, all lumpy and sour. I had a pile of those small, individually wrapped parcels which were slices of bread that Evie had wrapped together and put outside my room. I don't think I had eaten any of it since I had arrived. Evie explained that she still had a duty of care, because there was a Care Order and she was expected to provide minimal food items. So whether I ate it or not, it would be at my door every day I lived there.

She congratulated me on how well I had been getting on with the other house mates. Little did she know it was turning into a bit of a drugs den. Almost everyone there did drugs of some kind. The kitchen had become a place for the preparation of drugs, or for making special meals or tea out of Magic Mushrooms or whatever new thing we could find that gave us a buzz. It was our way of dealing with things. We didn't give any consideration to what it might be doing to our health, or if there were long term effects. Well you don't think when you're 15, do you? I did worry once though, when I had been asleep for over three days solid and no one noticed. I could have been dead for all anyone knew.

Chapter 26

The loud knock on my door got my attention. No one ever knocked on my door, especially Evie.

"Mail," she called out.

"Wow! Now that is novel," I said taking the small blue envelope and closing the door. "Thank you."

The letter was marked with a stamp saying it had been opened and checked. That aroused my interest straight away. *Well, you don't see letters stamped that way very often,* I thought. It was from Dave. He had been detained in a military prison. I had to read it twice for it to sink in. *Why on Earth would he be in prison?*

The letter went on to explain that he had smoked some weed on the night we were supposed to meet in Leicester, and how he was sorry. *Blah, fucking Blah.* He said nothing actually happened with the girls, they were just friends. *Sure, does he think I'm stupid?* Because he rarely did dope, he said it totally blew his mind. He had been AWOL--absent without leave--in order to meet me.

By all accounts the police had recorded the phone number I had on me and figured out I had written down his friend's number and traced Dave there. I had a rush of guilt. I never thought for one moment he would have gone AWOL to be with me. The guilt didn't last long though. *Well! Serves him right for not turning up to meet me when he should. If he had met me as arranged, he wouldn't have got caught, would he? We could have been happily living together now, away from all the crap, if he had just kept his side of the bargain.*

The letter went on to say he had spent ages trying to get hold of me and that he had finally managed to get in touch with Albert. Albert wrote back to him and gave him my address. The letter was full of mushy stuff, but I had moved on and it had been almost six months since that fateful night in Leicester. *Does he really think that I'd still be waiting?* I didn't even reply. What was there to say?

When I came back after going out for a walk up the beach, there was a letter under my door. It was from Lilly. She had rang Evie and asked her to tell me that she was finally free from her grounding, so I got busy planning our next weekend away. The Canterbury lads were all looking forward to meeting Lilly, they had heard so much about her. She must be nice, she was my friend after all.

We were on our way to the local youth club, coke and crisps were cheap and it was somewhere to hang out. The roads were a bit icy but that never stopped us going anywhere. I was riding pillion to J and we were coming up to a sharp bend in the road. The next thing I knew I was being dragged along the ground on my back by the scooter. I didn't feel any pain, but I remembered grabbing air and trying to reach for something, anything. The road beneath me and my trapped leg were going so fast, I was unable stop myself. But before I knew it, the scooter stopped sliding on the grass bank at the side of the road. *Amazing how despite the speed it felt like everything was in slow motion!*

I remained trapped under the scooter and in some pain. It took a while for me to realise what happened. My mouth must have come in contact with the road at some point because my two front teeth were broken in half. I asked someone, "Where are my teeth?" I also remembered J standing there with his hands on his head aghast, mumbling something about no insurance. "Look at the state of my scooter," he cried.

Never fuckin' mind the state of your scooter. What about me?

Some strangers tried to pull the scooter off my leg. I was shouting to make them hurry. It really wasn't helping, but I was in a bit of a panic. I let out a scream as the scooter was lifted, my leg still attached. One of the mirror rods had gone all the way through my knee. I took one look and passed out!

The Ambulance driver was beside me when I came around, telling me to breathe through the mask. I don't know how they got the rod out of my leg, but by the time I arrived at the hospital most of it was gone. I thought, *Where the hell is J?* I remembered Lilly calling my name and sitting in the ambulance, then I saw Lilly's parents at the hospital. I could hear them outside my room telling Evie I could stay with them until I got better, asking, "Where is her family?" I made a mental note to ring Alex and say hello. It must have been a year since I had spoken to him, and that was like trying to pull teeth.

I was discharged from hospital the next day following observations and after they removed a piece of rod out of my knee. X-rays revealed a small piece remained in my leg so I was given a local anaesthetic into my knee and they dug in there and pulled it out. I didn't feel much. After the doctor checked me over again, I was taken to Lilly's house.

Lilly's parents were lovely. They were always kind to me, but secretly I suspected they hated the influence I had over their daughter. They had me to stay for almost two weeks until I was able to get around and look after myself. After that, they dropped me off at my little pad. Lilly's mum had done a bit of shopping for me, so I didn't have to worry about food for a while.

Evie's persistent knocking on the door woke me from my nap. The pain killers were nice as they made me feel very calm and I slept a lot.

"There's a guy keeps riding his scooter up and down up front," she said. "I'm guessing it's for you as he is wearing one of those parka things."

I stood and looked out of the window but whoever it was had gone. There was no one there I knew. Evie left me to it and I started to doze. I soon heard the beeping sound of a scooter's horn. It pains me to say so, but it sounded like a child's bike. I stood up again to look out of the window. It took me a second to register that the face looking up at me was in fact, Dave. Dave? Dave! Panic rushed through me from head to toe.

"Oh shit!" I shouted, running around, doing my hair and putting on makeup. *What am I doing?* I thought. I hobbled downstairs.

I walked up to the scooter parked outside, held my hands out and shrugged, "Well it only took you six months to find me."

He got off his scooter and took off his open-faced crash helmet. His scooter looked lovely, metallic blue, and his crash hat matched. His last scooter had been white and showed off every bit of dirt.

"I've been staying at a campsite nearby waiting for you. No one knew where you disappeared to, only that you had been in an accident. I didn't want to go to the hospital just in case I got you in trouble." He waffled on.

"Okay, well that's the last two weeks, what about the five and a half months before that? You went to army prison for three months which leaves two and a half months by my calculations."

"Let's walk." He nodded in the direction of the beach and started to walk along the seafront. I don't know why, but I followed.

"You didn't reply to my letter?"

"Well you roasted me in Leicester didn't you?"

"I told you what happened."

"That wasn't a reason. Did you expect me to swallow that crap? You left me there alone! I didn't have anything to say to your letter and I still don't."

"But I love you Abbie, I've always loved you. It just took me a while for me to realise it."

"It's too late Dave. There's too much water gone under the bridge." As much as it killed me being so tough with him, I knew I had to be.

"Please Abbie," he pleaded, his blue eyes begging me to change my mind.

We sat in silence on the beach for about an hour, saying nothing else just watching the sea. Looking up at the night sky lit by the amusement arcades, Dave put his arm around me.

"I am so sorry," he whispered.

You might say, I started to thaw. I snuggled in close and inhaled the familiarity of him. I loved it.

"Hungry?" he asked.

"No."

We walked along the beach to the arcades then stopped in a café for some food. After watching him eat for a while, having not been hungry myself, I just hugged my mug of coffee. When Lilly suddenly came bouncing in with a few of the guys, I introduced Dave. We made our excuses and left. For some reason I didn't want to share Dave with anyone, I guess I felt we needed to be alone.

A huge part of me wanted to ask him to stay, or even say I would go with him wherever he wanted. But I knew we were no good together. I couldn't trust him. He sat perched on the edge of his scooter and pulled me into him, holding me close.

"You know where to find me if you need anything, including me." He wrote his parents address on a piece of paper and handed it to me. He put his hands up cupping my face and stroking my hair like he was trying to lock me away in his memory. Then he put on his crash hat and started his scooter.

Why do I do this to myself? I want to go. Why don't I? I will. No, I won't. I really don't know. All I knew for sure was I had feelings for him but I couldn't trust him. He had let me down and I couldn't forgive him for that. *I'm bad news too.* He had lost his army career because of me, what else would he loose if I went with him? I was so confused, and I felt that everything I touched turned to stone.

I watched him drive away

❧

"OH--MY--GOD!" shouted Lilly when I walked in the café the next morning, "Who the hell was he?"

"Dave."

"What? 'THE' Dave?"

"Yes 'THE' Dave, now shut up about him, it's over."

"Well if you don't want him, can I have him then? I bet he's good shag!" She giggled leaning over and pinching some toast off my plate.

"Lilly! Oh my god, have you got no morals?" I laughed. "Anyway, he's long gone."

Chapter 27

The wounds were healing nicely on my legs and only left a small battle scar. I found out the accident was caused by an American Diplomat driving on the wrong side of the road. Apparently he sent a message to the hospital with flowers saying how sorry he was. I didn't really remember it though, the pain killers were pretty strong.

I spent a lot of time in my room on my own whilst I got better. My knee was a bit stiff and the scabs began falling off my arms, but I wasn't happy in my own company. I hated being alone. It gave me far too much time to think. Although I hated being told what to do, I'd rather that than being alone. I couldn't win really, I hated it either way. I would seek out company. Sometimes I could remember what I had done and other times I couldn't.

That was how I met Adam. He was hanging around with some friends and asked if I wanted to go out for a drink? Before I knew it we were seeing each other and planning to move in together, even though he really was not my type and it had only been a few weeks. After a chat with Evie, I decided that I wanted a career with horses so I sought out an equestrian centre near Adam's place.

It was a big yard with lots of horses, a jumping yard but a riding school too, so lots of variety. They watched me ride two different horses, then said, "Okay, the job is yours." They said that I was bit rusty and needed fine tuning, but my "natural talent" was good and could be developed.

I ran to Adam hugging him. I was so pleased with myself and couldn't wait to tell someone.

"With some work I can get qualified to teach," I squealed excited. I was chuffed to bits.

"Not bad," Adam said with a nod of approval.

I moved in above the stables after a few days. It was freezing cold and smelt of horses but it was home to me, and I loved it. We had to be up at 6:00 am every day to see to the horses. We would put them out and feed them, then at 7:30 we got called into the house for breakfast, porridge or bacon sandwiches. The days were long and hard work, but I loved every single minute. Working with horses seemed to be the only way I could lose myself and the only place where I didn't seem to hurt inside.

I was so busy I didn't think about my past very often. I had started to forget a lot of things; other things were confusing to me if and when I gave them any thought. I would sometimes think about Molly and baby Kassie or the others, but for the most part I didn't allow myself to think about the bad stuff. It got hidden away somewhere in my head. No one knew, only me, and who would believe me if I told them anyway? *Best left where it is.* For a long time I blamed myself for the stuff I remembered. I must've deserved it, I must have been a really bad kid.

Horses blocked most of it out, but still I would do things and say things and not really know why? I was such a nasty bitch at times. *Why?*

I threw myself into my job and worked really hard with the horses. There were never any complaints about me. I could climb on any horse and I was becoming a good teacher. I started seeing more and more of Adam. In fact I stayed at his place more often than not. He was becoming more and more possessive, even overbearing, and it became harder to say no to him, so in the end I would just give in. He wanted me to stay at his place and he would take me to work and pick me up.

I rang Alex one day. I wanted to tell them all how well I was doing, I wanted them to be proud of me. Neither dad nor Maggie were at home.

"They're on their honeymoon," Alex said. The words rang in my ears like I had just been belted around the head again. *Honeymoon? Married?.... Married?* I couldn't believe it.

"How come? Why wasn't I told?" I whined at Alex. "Why wasn't I invited?"

"You were."

"When?"

"They wrote to you and gave the letter to Albert."

"Where's the letter then? It hasn't arrived!"

Then it clicked. Maybe they wanted to invite me, but I hadn't told them where I was. I hadn't spoken to them for months, but then, "It works two ways!" I shouted at Alex. I finally blew my stack and told him off, "Not one of you are bothered with me. I covered for you for years. I took beatings for you and you can't even be arsed to find out if I am alive! Thanks a fuckin' lot Alex, I love you too!" I slammed the phone down.

There were no tears, only anger. I felt left out as usual, but then why should they want me there? I was the black sheep, the one they handed away like a sack of rubbish. I didn't know where to turn in order to ease the pain. Adam tried to talk to me and all I wanted to do was scream at someone and tell them I was really a nice person. I wanted to tell someone I have to protect myself because no one else will. But if I told them that, I would have to tell them all the truth and then it would come out. I swore to Molly I would never tell. Now I wished I hadn't made that promise. But then she was still having to deal with mum, and I wasn't. I had escaped the torture chamber and she hadn't. I couldn't risk making it worse for her.

I lay in my room that night listening to the horses munch on hay in the stables below. I didn't want to see Adam tonight. I knew he would just try and make me feel better. He would think I would want a cuddle or, even worse, he might think sex would cheer me up. I couldn't risk it so I told him I had an early start and wouldn't be staying overnight. He got pretty angry. He hated me saying "No" to him, he was so possessive.

As I lay there, I wondered why it hurt me so, the fact dad had gotten re-married. I mean, I hadn't seen them for a year and before that, when I did see them, all I did was cause trouble. I could feel myself sinking into that familiar place of feeling sorry for myself, so I snapped out of it. I wasn't going to be the one to lie there and whimper any longer. I wasn't going to allow myself to become angry either. Anger was my way of dealing with most things, but, of course, I had little or no control when I got angry. It meant someone else usually got hurt, normally the person closest to me and on this occasion, it was Adam.

"I don't want to see you anymore," I said.

"What do mean? What are you talking about?" Adam couldn't speak quickly enough.

"Don't push it Adam, I really can't be doing heavy relationships right now."

"Heavy?" he shouted. "For fuck sake Abbie I haven't seen you in days!"

"Yes and you keep pestering me. I told you I just want to be left alone."

Part of me felt sorry for Adam, but he wasn't what I wanted. I didn't know exactly what I wanted, but I knew it wasn't him. So as much as it hurt him, I had to be cruel and tell him to get stuffed and leave me alone. The funny thing is, I didn't feel sad, I felt instant relief. It was like I didn't realise how much I had been controlled until I wasn't with him. A heavy burden fell off my shoulders.

It was difficult for awhile. I couldn't see the usual crowd because Adam would be there hoping I would show. So at weekends I would go to London on the train and see who I could meet. I would get stoned or pilled up and then go home on Sunday. Home was the stables. I was on my own, although skating on thin ice as I was forever getting back late or feeling ill after a bender. Adam was no longer there to keep me on the straight and narrow.

It was all I could do to stay away from Adam. Everywhere I went he turned up. I felt like he was seriously stalking me, but of course, he always showed genuine surprise to cover up. At times he actually got scary. He would think of an excuse to see to me and then ask me to have him back, telling me how he would change, constantly begging. He would plead with me saying how he would be anything I wanted. He would change just for me.

What doesn't he understand about the word, No? He could never be what I wanted. How could he, when I didn't even know what I wanted? The last and final straw was when I got back to the stables on a Sunday night. Looking out of the window as I closed the curtains, there he was hiding near the tractor. He would have had to climb the gates and snuck around to get there without the dogs hearing him. I ran to the next room and woke one of the stable lads in a panic. He ran outside bearing a pitch fork and chased Adam off. I hoped it would be the last I saw of him.

Good fuckin riddance too, Weirdo!

Chapter 28

I wasn't going to keep my job for much longer. The head girl said, "You're unreliable and can't be trusted. The horses can't look after themselves."

She was very sarcastic every time she spoke to me. I wasn't about to say, *Sorry I'm late. I got totally stoned last night and wow, am I ever feeling it today!* So I just told her, "Get stuffed! You're picking on the wrong person."

All hell broke loose! I don't know what came over me. It was like my blood boiled over and I was no longer in control. I saw red!

"You're just a dirty slag," she said.

That was it. I am told that I flew at her punching and kicking. I grabbed her hair pulling her head down so her face kissed my knee. Blood went everywhere as her nose exploded. I really didn't know what I was doing, but by the time I did, it was far too late. The damage was done. I had been blinded by my temper and scared too. *What if no one had been there to stop me? I could have killed that gobby bitch!*

Instead the owner screamed at me, "Get out of my yard! Get out I said!" as she pointed at the gate.

"What about my stuff?" I asked. "I'll go when I've got my stuff."

"Get out right now or I will call the police!"

A crowd of stable staff started to form along with people having their riding lessons. All stopped to see what was going on. I walked out to the gate and waited. I didn't know what else to do or where to go. A few minutes later the owner marched over with a black bin bag in her hand.

"There's your stuff. Now get out before I really do get the police involved." She threw the bag at my feet, turned and walked away.

As I walked along the road I didn't have a clue. *Where am I going to go? Everyone I know has someone. Every child and every person needs someone*, I thought, *just one person to believe in. I don't even have that.* Sure, I had plenty of people who used me for my popularity, for sex or for money, but I didn't have any real friends.

I just walked and walked. I struggled with the heavy, black bag so I found a hedge and took some of my gear out and stashed it in the bushes. It was hidden well enough for me to come back for it at a later date.

I was racking my brains where to go? All I could think of was Lilly's house, but I hadn't seen her for ages. I thought we were growing apart. She lived a bit of a journey away and could never come out when I was free. As I had got busier with the horses and going out every weekend, she spent more time at home. Her parents kept her pretty close at hand during the exam period. I wandered around Canterbury for most of the evening before bumping into some people I knew.

I was easily persuaded to go back with them for a few drinks and a party. When I got there though, I found my way to the bathroom and sat on the floor with my back on the door. What the hell am I going to do now? I had nothing and no-one. I thought about everyone that I could possibly use to help get me out of this situation. I even thought about going back to London. I loved the hustle and bustle there, the way that everyone just blended in. I didn't stand out there. I never had much money. I spent it almost as quick as it was given to me. I hadn't been on a good wage with it being a training position, so I had nothing saved. I didn't want to shag my way round London for money. I decided to take a chance and go home and see if dad and Maggie would have me back, so I rang Alex.

"Hi Alex, can you come and pick me up? I need a ride bro."

"Where to sis?"

"I want to come home."

"Home?" his voice all of a sudden went to a higher note.

"Yes Alex, Duh! Home!"

"Well, I don't know if dad will have that. They aren't here right now. Away until Thursday. Why don't you find a mate to crash down with till they get back?"

"Why don't you stop prattling around? I don't have much time. Please Alex, come and pick me up." The phone went silent for what seemed like ages. The silence killed me. Did he hang up?

"Uhhh. . ."

"Alex? Alex! Are you there?"

No reply.

"Alex! Will you answer me, please?"

"Okay, okay where are you then?" he mumbled.

I could tell he wasn't overly impressed with the idea, but thankfully he gave in. He owed me big time. *He's coming to get me,* I thought. *I can relax, a little bit anyway.* It took him just under an hour to show. I thought he would never arrive.

"You look in a right state," was how I was greeted.

"Yeah, well you're no oil painting yourself, Alex."

"Long time no see Sis. Hop on."

Swinging my leg over his scooter, I felt totally at ease. The icy wind bit my face as we sped along the dual carriageway to home. I was glad Maggie and dad weren't going to be there. I wouldn't want them to see me like this, a musty stable-hand out of work and down on my luck.

The sound of the scooter could quite easily have sent me to sleep. It purred just like a room full of hair dryers, as scooters always did. I daren't tell Alex though. I think he might have deposited me by the side of the road if I had called his beloved scooter a hair dryer.

I clung on to the scooter with one hand and held onto the remains of my black bag with the other, propping it between my stomach and Alex's back. I looked at the bag and asked myself, *Is that all I'm worth? A few dresses, shoes and handbags? Is that all there is?* I had stuffed a couple of dresses and jackets in the bushes, but the more I thought about it, the less likely I was of ever seeing them again. I had my makeup bag and a few toiletries and that was my total net worth.

I thought, *I'm a total failure!* I had caused everyone so much trouble and there was not much I wouldn't have and hadn't already done to get by. I wanted my own life and Albert got it for me. I had my own place and I blew that too. I had my dream job and I wasted that. I just hoped Maggie and dad might take me back or that would be it for me.

Suicidal? Understatement! I had no other choice. I had thought long and hard about ways to end my life before, and I had decided to go off a cliff. Yeah, that would be dramatic, like in the film *Quadrophenia*. I could relate to that movie. It all had gone wrong in my life too. I knew I wasn't to blame for all of it, but most of my trouble was that I didn't know when to shut up and walk away. The truth was, mostly, I didn't know when to ask for help.

We pulled up outside dad's council house. I couldn't call it home anymore and it didn't feel like my home. I hadn't lived there in over a year. I looked up at my bedroom window and smiled while I remembered climbing out of it to go out with my mates. Although I was a cow, I had to admit, I had guts, or was it stupidity? Or maybe in hind-sight, it was self-destruction.

In a way they didn't feel like my family anymore. Alex seemed a stranger to me now. Once upon a time we were so close. Maybe we were close when he needed me, but as soon as he didn't and wasn't getting beat up anymore, I was redundant. He might not have needed me now, but I needed him, and I despised him deep down for abandoning me. *Wow, dad had married Maggie. Where do I fit into this family? Will I ever fit?*

Chapter 29

"No way, absolutely No Way!" I heard the voices outside. Alex had gone out to meet dad and Maggie at the car to warn them of my arrival. Alex made me promise not to tell them he had fetched me home. *I can't believe I'm covering for him again, so HE doesn't get in trouble.* What could I say though? He had just rescued me in my time of need, eh?

The voices faded as I sank into a whirlpool of self pity. I stood in my room and looked in the mirror as a dark veil fell over me. In the depths of depression, I started to cry. Tears of indignation poured down my face. *I never cry! What's the hell's the matter with me? I don't even know who I am! Who is that person with the shitty tears and dripping mascara?* I stared into my own eyes and looked deeply into the reflection of my soul. It scared me. *I look like a ghost!* All the scars and imperfections from the life I had lived accented my mental scars and pulled me down hard. *I look like a deadbeat drug addict, raked out of the gutter and hung out to dry. What have I become? A nobody? I have nothing to prove I'm a somebody. No trophies, no ribbons, no awards, nothing really to make me proud. I got nothing but bad memories and a chequered past.*

I tried to smile through the tears at that old, familiar feeling of trying to compete with Alex. *He was always brighter than me at school, sly at home too. Let's face it, he must be the clever one, to get me to take the blame for him all the time. I'll never be a somebody like Alex. I'll never be good enough. It seems I spent all my time and energy digging a hole for myself that, maybe, I should just climb into and go to sleep.* I started to sob as sour thoughts took over my being. *Sometimes it feels as if I'm suffocating, slowly numbing to the pain. I can see the beauty in this life when others can't. I mean I love everything to do with nature, but I end up destroying it. In the end it just makes me want to scream because I know, I know life will slip away. I can stand in the rain, feeling every single drop hitting my skin. I feel it, deep inside my heart, mourning every lost accomplishment, every failed goal and every withered friendship. I feel it and it's coming again, raining on me like a cloudburst. What have I become? What have I always been? Why does no one want me? Is there any way out? So many questions, but never any answers. Everyone has slipped from my grasp, those who were once my friends, or perhaps never were. I should have never made a single friend, because every person I met eventually deserted me. They may have promised not to hurt me, but they always did and I hurt them back. Always!*

I was staring at myself crying like a child. *I hate me! I put on weight, my hair needs a cut and my skin looks like hell warmed over.* I turned away from the mirror in disgust. *I used to take so much pride in how I looked.* I glanced in the mirror again. *If I don't like what I see, how can anyone else like me? But, is that truly me? That witch? I honestly don't know.*

I looked at my reflection again, wondering why everyone wanted to leave home when they got older. *What's the point of going off in the world anyway? What am I trying to achieve? Happiness? It doesn't last, nothing does. I've proven that, not even love. Love never lasts. And all those friends you make along the way. They'll eventually ignore you, and then they will just fade away, they always do. Most of the time you don't even see it coming. But in the end you know. I learnt a major lesson or two a long time before I reached 16. Everyone goes away in the end!*

And I know why? Out of all things, I finally understand. It's because they can't stand being around me. I don't blame them. Why would they? Look at me! I don't even feel alive. It has to be because of that, there is no other reason. I am disgusting. I heaved in despair and wiped my eyes with the back of my hands. I started to gather my things. *I don't know where I will go. I don't know where I will go. I don't know where I will go,* like a broken record. *"Maggie please let me stay!"* I pleaded with her in my head. *I don't dislike Maggie, although I know she dislikes me. What am I thinking? I don't stand a chance. Why on earth did I think about coming back here anyway?*

"Abbie, you'd better get yourself down here," dad shouted up the stairs.

I had a rush of adrenaline, panic ran right through me. All the time I wasn't called I could hide in my room. It still looked the same, the same cream wallpaper, my posters on the wall of The Jam and Paul Weller. My record collection was still on the side and my row of Enid Blyton books sat on the chest-of-drawers unopened since last year. It was the same carpet, pale green with cream swirls. It was my room and I didn't want to leave it. *This IS my home!* I stood up and looked around my room and picked up my bag just as dad shouted at me again.

"I'm coming, be there in a tick," I called down. I walked out of my room and made my way downstairs, adrenaline rushing through my body. I could feel my hands tremble. Alex looked at me and shrugged his shoulders before grabbing his keys and walking out the door. I walked through the living room and followed him.

"Where are you going?" Maggie said sarcastically.

"What's the point?" I replied. "I didn't come here to argue."

"Why did you come here then?" dad chirped in.

"Because I have nowhere else to go. This is my family." I looked them both in the eyes, and they looked at each other. I could feel my eyes burning but I wasn't going to cry again. Either they wanted me there or they didn't, there was no point crying about it.

"Come and sit down, let's talk," dad said.

"Oh! Congratulations on getting married. Did you have a nice dress Maggie?"

"Thank you, and yes I did. I wore a lovely suit, but there's plenty of time for you to see the photos. Right, on to the RULES!"

"Rules?" I questioned, taking a deep breath, sighing out loud.

"If you're staying there has to be rules. We don't want none of the crap you used to give us young lady, no violence, no stealing and no running away," dad said.

I couldn't believe my ears. I could stay? I was over the moon. I would have agreed to anything. I didn't for the life of me think it would be that easy to move back home. I would have done it months ago had I known. It was weird though. I couldn't figure why Maggie agreed to have me back. I could still feel the tension when I was around her. I think she hated me ever since I was 11. Our relationship was tenuous, but I was home. *I'm home, I'm home, I'm home!*

The days went quickly. Maggie notified the school that I would be back to sit my exams. She thought that if I took them, an F grade would be better than a U, so I went along. I was never comfortable though. I felt like she was always waiting for me to trip up. I walked on eggshells. I felt she wanted me to make a mistake so she could throw me out. I had been to the precipice and looked over the edge. I didn't want to go there again, so I swore I would follow the straight and narrow.

I arrived at school according to the time table for exams. A lot of kids gave me funny looks like I had no right to be there. They had to be at school day in and day out to be able to take exams, and I had taken the year off, out raising hell.

The school hall was set up in rows of seats, a large clock on the wall in front ticked away the 45 minutes allowed for the paper. I did my best but science was never really my strong point.

I attended every exam. Maggie personally drove me to school to make sure I did. Some of the time I just sat and gazed out of the window, not thinking about anything really, just drifting off to some place foreign. I would wonder about Molly and the others and what they were up to. I hadn't seen them in such a long time. *I bet I could walk past them in the street and not recognise Daniel or Debbie.* I hadn't seen them for nearly six years. Molly had said they didn't want to see us because they were jealous of our lives. *Jealous? Huh! If only they knew.* I didn't think they would want my life for a second. *One day I will see them again and tell them, but for now I have to sort myself out.* I was going to do my best to turn things around.

I still struggled with drink and drugs even though they had no idea. I thought Maggie had guessed one day when I had taken a pill and drifted off while in the bath with the bath water running hot. I severely burnt my leg. I had to have melamine dressings changed for weeks after that but I still didn't get found out. That is until Maggie came home from work to find me paralytic on the couch. I think she thought I had a bad stomach bug at first until she smelt my breath. It was a close call, but Maggie let it go. I think she was more amused at how ill I had made myself and figured that I had taught myself a lesson. I had, if I wanted any chance of a family I had to stop.

I didn't drink again.

Chapter 30

I tried hard to keep my side of the bargain. I attended school to do my exams, I did my best to be in on curfew and I didn't steal anything, well apart from the odd ciggie. I tried to conform to the rules, even though at times I could have so easily walked out.

I hunted for a job but couldn't find one. Although there were a few riding schools nearby, none of them were looking to hire, not at a training level anyway. I was forced to join a Youth Training Scheme--YOP. They were the rage at the time. The only placement I could get was at Woolworths where I earn't £25 a week. Not a lot of money really, even back then, but at least it bought me some cigarettes. Often dad would give me a packet, but if he didn't I'd pinch them, always hoping he wouldn't find out. I thought the job would tide me over until something better came along, but I hated it. I hated wearing the red and white striped uniform. I was often late but they didn't say much, probably because I was cheap labour. My manager was horrible too. She thought she had a god given right to speak to everyone like they were a piece of dirt. *If anyone needs a smacking it's her!*

To be honest I thought I was far better. *I shouldn't be working in a shop, I should be outdoors working with horses. Why did I have to lose my temper at the yard? I had the job I wanted and tossed it.* I got fed up with tidying the magazine rack. I gazed out of the shop window and saw a familiar face. *Adam? Oh my god! Shit! I can't believe it.*

I ducked quickly behind the shoe rail. *How did he find me? Oh hell! Now what do I do?* I told my manager that I felt ill and asked if I could go home. After grabbing my bag and coat, I snuck outside and attempted to hide among the people in the town centre. I failed miserably. I think all I managed to achieve was making a pretty good fool of myself trying to get away. As Adam's scooter revved up, I knew there was no point, so I turned to face him.

"What don't you understand about the word 'No'?" I scolded then turned and marched away.

"I need to talk to you Abbie," he called after me, pushing his scooter alongside.

"There's nothing to say. I have nothing to say. I told you we're finished."

"I won't let you go Abbie, ever," he sounded weird.

"Well you have a bloody long wait then, haven't you?" I tried to be as cold as ice. I found it easy to be nasty to him. Anyone watching would've thought I was a right bitch and they would've been correct. I didn't want him anymore. He had his uses and they were no longer needed.

Who told him where I worked? I asked myself. *I'm going to flip if it's Alex!* I fumed away silently.

I caught my bus home, constantly looking out of the window with a nervous eye. He followed the bus. I started to feel scared, so I planned to not mess around, but get straight home and let Alex sort him out. When I got off of the bus I looked around for the scooter but no one was around. *Thank gaud for that!* I whispered, *Who does he think he is?*

I marched up the road to home and rounded the corner stopping in my tracks. He was standing there, outside our house. *Must've known the shortcut,* I thought, *Shit!* I ducked back around the corner and ran to the back of the houses. I climbed the fence and crept through our neighbour's gardens to the back ally which led to our house. I snuck in through the back door. I peered outside and saw him looking for me. I looked around for Alex but no one was home.

"Just great," I said out loud as I plopped down on the stairs, thumping the steps in frustration. I was trapped in my own home. If I went into the kitchen he would see me. If I went in my room he would see me there too. I was stuck in the back half of the house until somebody came home.

Looking around the edge of the curtain, I could see him perched on his scooter fiddling with his pockets and messing with his hair. Every now and then he glanced down the road. *He'll figure out soon something is wrong*, I thought. *It wouldn't take this long to walk home from the bus stop*. He must have read my mind. He put on his crash helmet, hopped on his scooter and raced off. I ran downstairs, wrote a note and stuck it on the inside porch door, in plain view so anyone could see. TELL ADAM, I DO NOT WANT TO SEE HIM EVER AGAIN! I couldn't be any clearer than that, surely. *What does it take to get through to him?* I sat on my bed wondering what to do if he came back? I decided to wait until Alex returned, then tell Adam to his face, again! Alex would back me up.

Maggie arrived home shortly after I had written the note. "What's this all about?" She shouted up the stairs.

I had no option but to tell her he was being a pain and wouldn't take no for an answer. I was being stalked.

"Well you do pick them," she said in her usual, "I told you so" voice.

"Pick what?" I instantly felt the hackles go up, it didn't take much. Maggie knew which buttons to press.

"Those wastes of space you hang round with, trouble makers the lot of them."

"Do you want to pick my next one then? Seeing as you're so good at it. Nothing I do is ever good enough for you is it?" I slammed the door behind me and sat on the stairs.

For a minute I thought, *What did I say? I can't afford to be homeless. But on the other hand, does that mean I should never say what I feel?* I was unsure as I walked back into the kitchen. Maggie had her back to me, feeding the cat. Domino was rubbing himself in and out of her legs, meowing his head off and acting like he was starving. We both giggled at the same time.

"Daft cat," Maggie said, putting his bowl on the floor.

"I'm sorry." I don't know where it came from, but there it was, probably the first apology of my life. Maggie tried to hide it but I could see a glimpse of shock in her expression. I quickly carried on talking to not allow her to savour the moment. "If he knocks on the door, can you tell him I'm not interested, please? I think Alex told him where I worked. He's been stalking me there. That's why I'm home early." For the first time ever, I managed to calm myself down.

"Ah! I see now," she nodded. "Now it makes sense. Don't worry I'll get rid of him," she assured me.

He didn't come back. I don't know if it was because he saw Maggie come home or if he finally got the picture. I had a couple hours or so to get ready for the "School leavers" disco. I can't say I was really excited, but a couple of girls in my year had asked me to go. *I have nothing else to do tonight, so why not?*

I pulled out my Dogtooth check miniskirt. It had a drop-waist and was very kind to my figure. I had started to lose a bit of weight now that Maggie was feeding me properly, and I wasn't eating all the junk food. I wore my black knee-length boots. They were the most comfortable ones I owned, bearing in mind I had a bit of a long trek up the huge hill to get to the school. Then I slipped on my fishnet stockings to finish off. After back-combing my hair and spraying half a can of hairspray to keep it in place, I looked in the mirror and surveyed the result, giving myself a twirl. *Ugh huh! I don't believe it, I look good!* I had my makeup done, nothing new, just the same old eyeliner. Glancing at the girl in the mirror, I said, "You'll pass!" I bounced downstairs and ran into Alex.

"On the way out, are you Sis?"

"Off to the school disco."

"Wow, living it large then!"

"Better than stuck in 'ere with you."

He laughed then shrugged, marched off and slammed the door. *A Town Called Malice* by *The Jam* blasted out of his room. We wouldn't see him again tonight. He liked to hide away up there. I heard Maggie tell dad he was still wetting the bed.

Walking up the hill, I had a strange feeling I was being followed. Trees either side of the concrete steps were moving in the wind. It's funny what you can imagine when you're on your own. My entire senses where on high alert. I couldn't hear anything much, I couldn't see anything, no footsteps behind me. All the same, the eerie feeling was there, so I quickened my pace. My heart was pounding. It was a hard enough hill as it was, never mind practically running up it, looking over my shoulder the whole way. *You're just being daft,* I thought. I could hear some girls giggling further up the hill. I knew I was almost there, almost up to where the street lights began.

I heard a cough not far behind. *I knew it! I knew there was someone there.* I ran the rest of the way, not daring to look behind. As I reached the top a few girls were hanging around the railings smoking and giggling. I tried not to look flustered but I guess they read straight through me. They didn't say anything but the silence and staring down the hill spoke volumes. I knew there was someone behind me, I'd sensed it, but I questioned whether or not I was over-reacting to the darkness of the night sky. It was spooky with the branches waving slowly in the evening breeze, creaking and groaning. I started walking faster to get away, but I heard footsteps running now. I started to panic and my heart was racing. Again I looked behind me, nothing. Maybe I was hearing things after all, relieved that I wasn't going insane.

The thumping of the school disco could be heard in the housing estate opposite the school. The flats were a meeting point full of kids having a sneaky fag where they couldn't be seen by anyone that might grass on them to parents. I hung around waiting for my friends. I didn't have to wait long and they suddenly appeared.

"Let's do it then girls," someone said. "Let's go partieee!"

Giggling, we ran over the road to the school. We all thought it was going to be full of kids, that there wasn't going to be any male talent. We were fairly sure of that, but it beat staying at home.

D.I.S.C.O. by *Ottowan* rang out. I wasn't a lover of this type of music and this had to be the cheesiest of the lot, so I hung around near the stage where they were selling crisps and coke. I was relieved when *Madness* came on next. A lot of the lads got up on the dance floor, dressed in two tone suits or Harrington jackets and straight jeans or Chino's. They pogo'd jumping into each other and sang away. It was quite amusing to watch but lethal if you wanted to join in.

The girls I met up with were flirting with some local lads that had come into the school to see what was going on. The boys were about 19, so the girls were hoping. I went outside for a ciggie. I couldn't bear to watch those silly girls flirt all night.

Chapter 31

"Please talk to me Abbie."

I twirled around with a sharp intake of breath. "Adam, oh my god, you scared me!"

"Will you talk to me?"

I knew he was serious, telling and not asking, *really annoying!*

"I told you last time, there is no WE. WE are over." I turned and started walking away when he grabbed me by the arm spinning me back to him.

"Get the fuck off of me!" I yelled as I yanked myself away. He let go checking around to see if he had been seen. There were a few people gathering outside and they were watching and whispering. I was used to causing a scene so I ignored it, but I'm glad they were there because it gave me my opportunity to walk away without too much fuss.

I went back inside the youth club to the disco and walked over by the stage near the Disc Jockey. *Imagination's* chart song *Body Talk* came on next. It got lots of people up dancing, even the DJ came down onto the dance floor. As I looked around, my friends were walking out of the door with the older lads waving at me, giving me a girly giggle wave goodbye.

Great! Now what? That's me dumped and left alone while Adam's outside! Just as I thought I had no hope of getting home without him following me, he walked in. I was really totally fed up now. I could feel myself starting to lose my temper and I threw him a warning look not to come near me. He edged away and stood near the tuck shop, propping the counter up. I moved to the other side of the hall where it was a little less crowded and started dancing. Yeah, I was on my own but I didn't know what else to do, and to be fair I didn't care.

There was a group of girls dancing around there handbags and a few other girls dancing with boyfriends. I moved over near the DJ who was still dancing away to *Imagination* and smiled at him. He looked around behind himself to check it was him I was smiling at and then smiled back at me. He seemed to be shocked I would smile at him. He wasn't the normal sort of guy I'd flirt with or dance with either. The first thing I noticed about him was how perfect his teeth were. I was always a bit conscious of mine since the accident but his were straight and white. I danced close to him for a while then he pulled me in.

He has a bit of a nerve. Who is he anyway? He was flipping lucky I didn't belt him one for his cheek. I had seen him around school. He had often looked at me but his tongue was out drawling when we had passed each other at school so I secretly knew that he liked me. All I knew about him was that he was in the same year.

I felt uncomfortable dancing with him though. Mods didn't do that sort of thing, especially in public, dancing that close and with a grebo too. A "soul head" we called them, no identity because they followed the crowd like sheep. If my friends could see me now my image would be all but done in. I committed mod suicide.

His arms were soft but strong and warm around me, gently pulling me in. Curling closer into the snug concave of his arms, I know I sighed. *I just hope he didn't hear it.* It seemed so wrong but so right, and I didn't even know his name. For once I was happy inhaling his soft scent as I looked up into his gorgeous hazel eyes. The feelings were so real. I had never felt that way before and certainly not with a stranger. *What is he doing to me?* Realisation hit me of the purity of the moment, and I would treasure it forever. Even if I didn't ever see him again, I would remember the feeling of security wrapped in his strong arms. I loved it but was scared by its speed and severity. *I might never feel this again,* I thought. *Is this what I've been longing for? Does it really exist?* A massive urge took over. I wanted to absorb him and keep holding on and never let go. I needed to know everything about him, because after I had felt such closeness, the world would be unbearably cold and lifeless without it.

"My name is Abbie," I looked up into his face searching his soul. He was about six feet tall with dark brown hair and olive skin. *Perfect skin,* I thought *and perfect teeth.*

"I know," he laughed, smiling at me. "Back in a tick, got to change the song." He ran up to the stage.

How did he know my name? I looked over and Adam was glaring at me. I could see the poison in his face. He was hurting watching me flirt away with the DJ, but did nothing, just stared.

The DJ came back and said, "Oh, my name is Lawrie, nice to meet you." He held out his hand.

I grinned and offered him my hand to shake his, in a jokey kind of way.

"Nice to meet you too."

We spent the evening together, laughing and dancing. I hadn't had so much fun in years. To be able to enjoy myself without worrying whether I looked cool was a first. The hours passed quicker than ever and before I knew it, it was time to go home. I really didn't want the night to end, it was all too magical. I had feelings rushing around my body I never knew existed. He gave me a lift home on his red 100cc Suzuki motorbike. That was a change too. I had never ridden pillion on a motorbike.

We sat outside my house until we couldn't take the cold anymore. I wasn't saying much just curled up in his arms keeping warm, taking in his scent and loving every minute of the silence. It was nice not having to fill the space with words that meant nothing, just being with him was enough.

We spent most days together for a few weeks, mostly riding around on his bike or he would come round to my place and play games on the Atari. Maggie didn't really like him, but then she didn't like any of my boyfriends.

"Can you come over to mine today," Lawrie asked on the phone. "We've got the flat to ourselves," he said cheekily.

"Oh great, are they out all day?"

"Yup! I'll hire a movie too, see you in awhile," he hung up and I ran to get ready.

When we got there his parents weren't in, so he gave me the grand tour of his flat and then we settled on the couch where we watched a movie together. All I remember after that was waking up laying on him. I quickly got up thinking of how awkward that must have been. Wiping my mouth, *did I dribble?* But he didn't say anything so we just laughed it off. I sat back down and we watched another movie holding hands.

It was getting late in the morning but that didn't really matter. We started to just talk after a while. Part way through a sentence he stopped and closed in on my face and kissed me. I sat there kind of expecting it and then he laughed and kissed me again. *This guy's cheeky, and I like it.* I kissed him back and then we started to get a bit intense. We moved into his bedroom and onto his bed clothes flying everywhere. He ended up on top of me and he put his hand up my shirt feeling around, which led to me taking off his shirt. One by one our bits of clothing found there way to the floor. Then he asked me nicely if I wanted to have sex with him.

"Yes!" I said. He didn't need to ask because for the first time in my life I actually wanted it to happen.

"Are you ready?" he asked.

"As ready as I will ever be."

"I love you, Abbie"

At first I thought, *That was quick!* But then I said, "I love you too." I knew I loved him straight away but I was afraid to say it.

Lawrie said he had fallen for me when I had started at the school. I hadn't really noticed him that much, but he noticed me and admired me from a distance.

"Are you okay, Abbie. . .are you okay?"

"Stop asking me if I am okay," I laughed. "I'm fine, honest."

He was so concerned he would hurt me, maybe because I froze I don't know. Although I can't say it was amazing having sex, it felt amazing being with him. It wasn't the sex, it was how he made me feel. After we finished we just lay there and cuddled while he told me how much he had always loved me and that whatever happened, he would always be there for me.

Yeah, I've heard that before. It all sounded and felt too good to be true.

The sound of keys in the front door brought us back to our senses a bit sharpish. In a fit of giggles we rushed around putting some clothes on before his parents came in.

Chapter 32

We sat there in the back row of the cinema, Lawrie snuggling up next to me. His arm was around the back of my seat and he pressed awkwardly against my leg. *Busy hands,* I thought. He was doing his best to grope my boobs with the one while pulling my left hand onto the bulge in his Jeans with the other.

"We came here to watch a movie," I snapped pushing his hand away.

He turned his head to me and said, "Abbie, don't you remember? I'm going away to college."

"Of course I remember."

"Well it's February already, and I only have until April. I love you Abbie, you're my best friend. Well actually, you're much more than that now."

"How could I forget?" I mumble. *I've been dreading this but I knew it was coming.* "Yes I do remember," I repeated.

After a pause he looked down at his feet, his face twisted in angst. He whispered, "Well, I have some bad news."

What can it possibly be? I wondered. Everything negative flew through my brain, as the pessimistic me took over. *Are we breaking up? It can't be that bad ,surely? I know I'm hard work* *and get jealous easily but. . .*I braced myself waiting for the all too familiar stab of pain.

"I'm leaving for Sea College on the fourth."

The initial shock resulted in a blank stare. *Sea college?* No tears, no sadness, just...nothing. I was completely stunned, reeling, crushed!

"I guess…I mean…what?" I mumbled trying to digest what I had just heard. "You're leaving for sea? In practically two weeks?" My tone of voice ran up the scale to a very high pitch.

"Yup."

"I guess it won't be that bad," I lied trying to hold my composure.

I couldn't even look him in the eye without fear of bursting into tears. Thoughts ran through my head like, *Will I ever see him again?* or *Will things ever be the same? I finally found someone to protect me and now he's gone. Okay, maybe he'll come back, but how can I ever be sure? I can't trust anyone.* There was nothing I could do. I just stood up and walked out of the cinema. I had to be on my own. He tried to reason with me that night, but I had nothing to say. I was hurting too much.

We spent a lot of time together over the next few weeks, making up for time to be lost. There was a lot of sex as we began to explore our love for each other. Before we knew it, the time had arrived.

We met in the park and took a long walk to say our goodbyes and pledged that nothing would keep us apart. He held my hand and looked me straight in the eyes when he promised that he would not leave me, ever.

"I believe you," I told him wanting to believe, but feeling sick with fear and worry.

How could it be? I knew the pain of hatred and abuse, but how could love be so painful. I hadn't realised until he left, that love could physically hurt like a punch in the stomach. I always thought "heartache" was just some fancy pretend word made up by romance writers. Yet the separation from Lawrie tore me apart so much that my heart literally ached. I was miserable, and once again I carried the weight of the world on my shoulders.

Sometimes I could still feel him on my lips. I would tell myself that I could put up with this small period of pain and so much more to be honest, to have him all to myself one day. As difficult as it was, I tried my very hardest to remain sane and not get jealous, but unless I heard from him every day I would panic. *What if he finds someone else? What if he changes his mind? I finally found true love and the thought of losing him is unbearable.* My jealousy caused arguments. *What, am I trying to drive him away?* Maybe my mind was thinking if I got rid of him now then it wouldn't hurt so much later. I was confused, but I had too much time to think and, as always, struggled to deal with anything and everything to do with love.

We wrote most days, telling each other how much we loved each other and planning after Sea school was finished. We were 16 years old and had just finished school. We tried so hard to make it work before he went away. It was difficult though because my parents weren't keen on him and his parents weren't keen on me. It was like we came from different planets, and we did. I was a mod and he was into normal chart music, although he did his best to dress like a mod when he came to mod dos with me.

I started feeling really weird and wondered if it was more of the pains of love. Every morning was the same. I would smell something from the kitchen, anything, and run to the bathroom gagging.

"Maggie, I need to talk," I murmured sheepishly in the kitchen. "I've got something to tell."

She cut me off, "Let me guess." Maggie had her usual know it all look. "Let me make it easy, I'll tell you what's wrong."

I nodded, looking down at my feet, thinking, *Will she kick me out?*

"You're pregnant!" she said in her usual, sarcastic voice. She sounded cocky, "I saw it days ago."

"Well why didn't you say something then," I snapped back.

Not once did it occur to me that my unborn child's father might not want it. After all, he loved me. He had told me so over and over. In my naiveté, I had made myself believe that sex was love. After all, I didn't sleep around all the time I was with Lawrie. Now I was excited about the idea of being a mum. *Me? A mum!*

I wrote to Lawrie, the new father to be, expecting, well hoping for him to share my enthusiasm. I thought he would want to rush right home, scoop me in his arms, profess his undying devotion and propose to me on the spot!

In the real world, he was a sixteen-year-old boy, getting a letter from a girl he barely knew, stating the scariest words a young man could ever hear, "I'm pregnant!" He should have been studying at Sea School and not having to worry about anything else. After all, we had only been seeing each other for a matter of weeks.

"Are you sure?" was his first question.

I was hurt right off. "Of course I'm sure."

"Are you sure it's mine?"

I was devastated. "Do you need to ask?"

That question stabbed me in the heart, and it also should have been a warning. I should have known something was wrong when he had doubts. But I had always been a romantic deep inside and I wanted, no not wanted, I needed to believe his pledge. I needed to believe in love so badly that I didn't process his doubts. To me, they were just a reaction to major news. *He'll come around.* I didn't realise though I was going to have to take on his entire family.

"How could you know so soon? Have you done a test?"

"No, but I just know I am."

How could I explain that I felt it inside? At the time I didn't realise that it was his mother saying all of the horrible stuff and putting ideas and seeds of doubt into his head. She told him how I slept around and that the baby could be anyone's.

I went to the doctor to confirm what I already knew. Yes, I would be a mum. Soon the tiny life inside would be in my arms.

Around my fourth month of pregnancy, when my belly started to get bigger and my breasts heavier, Lawrie and I began drifting apart. His family was too strong for him. To be honest mine were just as bad, filling my head with stuff because I had told them of his doubts. I wanted them to say he loved me, but no.

"He's no good," Maggie would say, "Don't waste your time."

I was heartbroken. I knew he loved me, but who was I kidding? This is ME we're talking about. Nothing is ever easy for me. What's new?

Chapter 33

I don't think it hit either of us, until I started to show. My tummy was evidence just how permanent this was. Once there was "proof," it dawned on Lawrie's mother that her son would be a parent with someone he neither really knew nor could truly love that quickly. I guess she felt she had to protect him. After all, he was still a kid, in her opinion.

"It's not yours," his mother would say. I know he tried to fight her but he didn't have the rebellion in him like I did. His family was secure, the same mum and dad and everybody still together. His was from a total different upbringing than mine, I mean as different as Yin and Yang!

With a rush of hormones raging through my body, I still clung to the juvenile notion that it had to work out. We had to be a family. We had created a little life together, another little person to love, and that had to mean something to Lawrie, like it did to me. If it didn't, then all of those carefully planned fantasies, all of those sweet little stories were lies. I really didn't want to, no I just couldn't believe that. I had created a perfect world in my mind, a world where there was a happy ending at the end of the rainbow, and it involved Lawrie and our unborn child.

Without Lawrie, it meant I would have to face reality, that there was no such thing as hope, that I was going to be a mum and I was going to have a child who would depend on me, alone. *Me? I can't even look after myself, how am I going to take care of a baby?*

All the fantasies in the world didn't prepare me for his fatal, last letter. "I'm sorry Abbie, it's over," he said. It hit me like a torpedo. His letters stopped coming and the phone didn't ring. I knew that was it. He was off to sea with no way for me to try and stop it. I had absolutely no control. I had to sit back and watch the breakup, alone. I never felt so helpless. I knew deep down inside that Lawrie wanted the baby. I knew that he wanted me, after all he had bagged one of the school's major catches. Well, so he assured me often enough. Why would he let me go without a good fight? *Did he fight? Maybe he did and lost.* All I knew was, I was pregnant and alone.

My heart was torn apart, and I could hardly breathe. I panicked and even considered having an abortion. But even if I did, would Lawrie be allowed to see me again? *I doubt it, his mum had made up her mind.* She's formed her opinions, right or wrong. I knew it would be a fight with her before I could have her Lawrie back. I didn't know what to do. I stayed in my house for weeks, sulking, slipping back into the depression that had so often consumed me. Lawrie had been first to lift the clouds of darkness and now he was gone. *What am I going to do now? Who will want me with a baby?*

I had a lot of planning to do. It didn't occur to me at first, but I soon realised that having the baby would be the one thing in my life that was all mine, the one person who would love me unconditionally. It took some time to figure out that this was the best thing that ever happened to me.

Maggie was convinced that I had gotten pregnant on purpose. I hadn't. I was on the pill, how could it be on purpose? I showed her the packet, but she still didn't believe me. I had taken them all, but what the Doctor didn't tell me, when I had been prescribed antibiotics for a chest infection, was that I needed to use additional protection. Nevertheless, there was no doubt in my mind, I knew I would be keeping the baby. I rubbed my stomach feeling the bump, a bump that was steadily growing inside me.

"I will look after you baby, don't worry," I told my stomach, gently rubbing it. "I'll be here for you, and I will never allow you to be treated the way I was as a child. I promise you that!"

Maggie came to ante-natal classes and all the midwifery appointments with me. We even started getting on a lot better since she told me I was pregnant. I could almost say friends. She helped me pick out baby clothes and advised me on what I needed. The social services gave me a grant to help buy things like a cot and a pushchair. Most of the items I bought were second hand, but the baby wouldn't know the difference.

Lawrie was neither seen nor heard of; he had no involvement at all, much to Maggie's pleasure.

"I told you he wouldn't support you, didn't I?"

She often waved the red flag in my face. She always had to be right. *Why can't she be wrong,* I wondered, *just this once?* I really needed her to be wrong. I left loads of messages for him with his mum. I heard he had left sea school and was now working on the ferries. He never returned a single phone call.

Appointments were every month at first and everything was perfect. I found out at 18 weeks that I was going to have a little girl. To say I was overjoyed, would be an understatement. Towards the end of my pregnancy, it got to the point where I couldn't get myself up if I sat down. My stomach was huge.

My due date was the 17th of February. My leap year baby wasn't far away and, when it passed uneventfully, I was in a ditch. I was so upset. At that point I didn't care how much pain labour and childbirth would bring, I just wanted it over and done. My baby girl refused to come out, and I kept counting the days. *Where did she get all this stubbornness?* Ten days later I was admitted to hospital to be induced.

I left another message with Lawrie's mum when I was in the early stages of labour. I asked him to come to the hospital if he wanted to be with me when she was born. He never came.

I was screaming in pain when my contractions were two to three minutes apart. My labour had been full on since the first contraction. An injection of Pethidine was given, and it didn't take long before I was in the land of Ga Ga. Ah yes, I did remember. I recognised this place, it had been a long while since I had been stoned.

Then they asked about my last bowel movement. How embarrassing! I had to do it on the bed where I lay. Talk about torture. Pain, pain, and more pain!

"Get it out of me!" I screamed at the poor midwife. I then received the hiding of a lifetime. They had to cut me down below and the pain was indescribable. She was coming so fast I was ripping. I didn't even have the chance to push and there she was, this beautiful little person I had been waiting forever to meet. There was no noise though, no cry, the room was manic, nurses and doctors running around. The baby was taken out of the room in a dreadful silence.

"Where is she? Why are they taking my baby?" I was getting in a right mess, shouting at Maggie who had been with me throughout the whole labour. It seemed like forever, that macabre silence then it finally came. "Whaaaaaaaa!" That cry was music to my ears and I breathed a long sigh of relief.

"She was sleepy from the Pethidine you had, it's all okay," the doctor assured me. "Baby is fine."

Again I tried to contact Lawrie. I spoke to his mum telling her how Lawrie now had a daughter and that she was a grandma and the baby was fine. I told her all about how beautiful she was with her mop of dark fluffy hair and how much she looked like Lawrie. She promised to pass on the message.

I had no idea what to expect really. Everyone had told me various stories or offered opinions and tried to put me off in the early days. I heard countless horror stories of giving birth, but to be honest it wasn't all that bad, especially when it was over. *Or is that nature helping me to forget the pain?*

I found it hard over the next few weeks. Maggie pretty much left me to it, but she was in reach if I needed her. It was about then that I looked at her and realised what a friend she was. She was my mum and I had just rejected her all those years. She had never done a thing to hurt me, I caused it all myself. *Am I growing up? Maybe it's maternal feelings.* I thought I was grown up, after all, I was a mum now. I had to think about the baby, not just myself.

I tried to forget Lawrie, but every time I looked at the baby I saw him. She looked so much like him. Everybody said it all the time too, so it wasn't just me. I couldn't escape it. I rang so often to speak to him, almost to the extent of becoming a stalker myself. It wasn't long though before I realised his mum wasn't giving him the messages.

It was always, "He is in bed," or "He is at work," or "He's nipped out." I think I heard every excuse under the sun as to why I couldn't talk to him. I guess I just wanted to hear from his lips that he wasn't interested. I needed to hear it from him personally and not his mum.

Chapter 34

"Everything is fine," the consultant said, pulling Lilly's hips around. It was the day of my post natal. The baby and I were getting checked to make sure we were both fine and healthy. Lilly lay there having a major temper tantrum. She screamed her cat like impressions informing the doctor in a very loud verbal manner that he should just leave her alone!

"Nice healthy lungs," he grinned, looking into her mouth and pushing her tongue down to see in her throat.

"All is well. Just go along to the baby clinic regularly to check on her weight. You're both doing great," he winked at me then left the room leaving me to calm her down. I dressed Lilly as her screams began to fade.

I named her Lilly after my friend. I guess she was probably the only true friend I ever had, my longest running friendship when times were tough. I appreciated her being there, I needed her much more than she needed me, but I never let on.

She was over the moon when I called to tell her about Lilly. She visited me in hospital and held the baby once, but I never did see her again. *I guess you can't exactly put a baby on the back of a scooter can you?* I had moved on and she left me to it. I wouldn't have fit into the "being cool" group with a pram in front of me. Funny how my perspective changed. Mods didn't seem so important now.

Some of the girls from Woolworth's called to say hello and offered to take me out to celebrate the post natal. It was the "beginning of freedom after childbirth," they said. I really didn't want to go, but Maggie persuaded me.

"You need some free space."

"No it's okay... I'm fine honest."

"You get yourself out and relax. Go on have some fun. You never know when the next time will be," she said with a furrowed brow, but in a jokey way.

"But.. ."

"You've got eighteen years of hard work ahead of you girl!"

"Okay, okay," I agreed, getting ready to go out. *The problem is I don't know who I am. I can't dress like a mod anymore. How can I be a mod and a mum? The two just don't mix.*

Maggie helped me out and lent me a dress to wear. It was pretty forgiving of a belly that was hanging around, loose and stretched from childbirth.

I looked at myself in the mirror. *I'm certainly not going to wow anyone tonight,* I thought raising my eyebrows. I stuck my tongue out at myself and left the room. I grabbed my bag, gave Maggie a hug and gently kissed Lilly on the forehead while she slept. Picking up the Polaroid's to show my workmates, I headed off on the walk into town.

"I'll pick you up at 1:00 am at the club," dad called after me.

"Okay, no worries," I said looking back at Lilly fast asleep in her carrycot in the living room.

"She'll be fine," Maggie smiled. "Now get going before I change my mind."

I felt lost walking into town, no baby and pretty much no belly. I felt alone again and I had only left the house two minutes ago. Already I was wishing the night would end. I considered turning back, but I knew that Maggie wanted to play with Lilly by herself without me watching her every move, just like any normal Grandmother would.

The music thumped away and the club was packed. I don't think I had ever been to a real nightclub, well, not one without sixties or soul music playing. The dance floor was heaving. *Visage* was playing *Fade to Grey* and lots of people were dancing like a hundred robots.

I felt a tug on my arm and was quickly ushered into the club with the girls from Woolworth's. I wasn't feeling up to dancing. The truth was I didn't know how to dance to this sort of music. I sort of shuffled around trying to still look cool and let people think I actually knew what I was doing. *Ain't No Body* followed, by *Rufus and Chaka Khan*. I loved that song and danced away forgetting everything for a minute. *It's Raining Men* was blended into the end of it, *The Weather Girls*. Everyone singing along, I knew the song. Dad used to tape the Top 20 on the radio every week and I would listen while I helped him clean his trucks out. *If only it was raining men!* I giggled to myself.

Photos of Baby Lilly were passed around, everyone oooing and ahhing over her locks of brown fluffy hair and big blue eyes. I had only been out for an hour and I missed her so much.

Looking around the dance floor I saw a few people I knew. Not many recognised me without my mod gear and black bitch lines. My hair was bleached and had grown quite a bit. It was a shock when I saw him. It wasn't too surprising that, although he looked right at me, he walked by and went and sat down without a clue. I stopped in my tracks. I couldn't believe what I saw. Lawrie was standing there, right in front of my eyes.

"What do I do?" I whispered to a friend, both of us looking his way. He must have felt our laser beam eyes burning a hole right through him. As his head moved up he looked directly at me. It took a few moments for him to realise who I was and finally he mouthed, "OH MY GOD." I grabbed the pictures off of my friend and marched right over to where he was sat. He looked shocked.

In true style he just said, "Hi, Abbie, how have you been?"

"How have I been?" I hissed. "I've been giving birth to your fucking daughter, that's what, and I'm fine thanks for asking."

"I…I didn't know," he stammered looking me right in the face.

I found it hard to be angry. I loved him so much, seeing him just confirmed it, but he hurt me big time. How could I ever forgive him for leaving me alone?

"Of course you knew, don't try that one, and here's your daughter." I threw pictures in his direction.

"A girl?" He didn't seem to know or he was a damn good actor. I threw more pictures of Lilly on the table in front of him and walked away. I needed to compose myself.

I stood at the bar shaking. Inside I was scared. I certainly wasn't expecting him here, of all people. *Well at least now he can't deny her existence,* I thought.

"I honestly didn't know," said a voice beside me quietly in my ear.

I turned around and Lawrie stood there. I had waited for this moment for almost a year and now the words wouldn't come. I paused, then I said, "I called you a thousand times and left as many messages with your mum. She knew all about it. I even rang you when I was in labour."

His face showed horror. I could see it was genuine shock too.

"She is beautiful," he smiled.

My heart melted straight away. It never did take him long to get to me.

"I know she is." I played with him, posing with my hands on my hips doing my best model impression. "Of course she's beautiful, she's mine after all."

Putting his arms around my waist he drew me in. I was back in the warm, strong arms of the one man I loved.

"She's mine too," he said gazing into my eyes. "From now on, she's mine too."

THE END

(Or is it the beginning?)

Epilogue

I could have gone on a lot longer with my story because the troubles didn't suddenly end when I got back together with my baby's father. But I have told you all I really need to tell. I wanted to try and convey that even when horrific things happen to you as a child, you can pick yourself up, dust yourself off and make a good life if you choose. I chose to be a survivor and not a victim. No, it wasn't easy, not for a minute.

With a great deal of pain and introspection, I have told it all in grim detail. After keeping such secrets for thirty years the telling has been therapeutic in one way and troublesome in another.

Lawrie and I stuck together much to our family's disgust-- at first--and we married when baby Lilly was four years old. She was my bridesmaid. I was pregnant with our second baby then too, and we are now blessed with two beautiful girls. We had to go it alone in the beginning and struggle through because everyone was against us. We moved in together one week after meeting up at the disco. Our families gave us an ultimatum, and we chose each other. Ahh, young love conquers all! We went and rented a bedsit and that's where we started. We made an awful lot of mistakes but the one mistake I didn't make was falling in love with Lawrie. It was the best thing I ever did.

I had pretty much stopped doing drugs when I met Lawrie. He helped me through a lot of issues and showed me other ways to deal with my pain. Over the years he has been both my hero and my saviour. He broke down all the barriers and taught me it was okay to cry. I was about 25 years old before I learned how normal people cry, and when I did, I didn't think I would ever stop. It was like Niagara falls. I cried when I was happy and cried when I was sad, just like other people do. Yup, I'm a prize winning crier now.

It seems like Lawrie has spent most of his life trying to make me happy. At times I know I'm still difficult, always burdened with my past. But then all the things that happened to me are what make me ME. Today I live on a farm with my own horses. I don't need to steal other peoples anymore to have a ride.

My step mother? Well, I have nothing to do with her and never want to, but I did tell her how I felt in person. I thought it would make me feel better when I told her how much she hurt me, but her denial of some things and how it would affect someone mentally just made me feel even more worthless. I was hoping for some closure and got nothing but pain. When she started to train to become a social worker, I panicked and wrote to the Social Services telling them truth. All of us kids did. How could she advise other families? She stopped training. I don't know if it was her decision or not, but it was for the best.

No, I didn't go to the police, engage the legal system, or try and press charges against Uncle Joe or mum. I couldn't even describe to you what he looked like some 30 odd years later or tell you his last name or the others. My mind has blocked most all of that out. I do remember the faces of the other kids though. I absolutely will never forget their screams of pain. I just hope they survived.

Abuse of children by adults still goes on everyday around the world. It creates shame, fear and confusion in a child and these emotions, in turn, produce silence. Silence is well known to be one of the pernicious fruits of abuse. It means that allegations most often surface many years after the abuse has ceased. Then it is too late for criminal proceedings to be successful. But--and there is a but--the victim needs to know that telling the secrets--sorry Molly--is the best therapy. The pain will never completely go away, but some of the hurt will fade leaving room for true happiness.

When I was writing this story, I hoped I might remember more, because there is a lot I can't fully recall, just snippets of horror. Much of it is all locked away in my safe place, thankfully.

My step sister, Molly, died when she was 33. She had become a serious self harmer. She attempted suicide so many times but always survived. She jumped off a bridge onto a dual carriageway and lived. She jumped off a hospital roof and had a lot of broken bones but lived. She even cut her wrists and her own throat and survived. Finally, she was sectioned and put into secure care where she hung herself whilst on ten minute suicide watch! She died leaving a son who will never know his father, because he was another guy that mum had set up. I don't think Molly ever knew what true love felt like, poor girl.

Looking back, I'm sorry I couldn't have been there for her. She couldn't walk away from her mum; all her life she kept going back for more. It sounds strange but I think she was addicted to the punishment. It was the only kind of love she knew. Molly was the kindest person you would ever want to meet. She would do anything for anyone but couldn't live with her own demons. She didn't deserve what she got, none of us did! I'm so thankful my dad took me away from that house of horrors.

Every single one of us is scarred. Debbie has had drink issues and suffers with nerves and depression. Daniel has been in and out of prison for drugs and violent offences. Alex too has serious problems with alcohol. He still has problems dealing with emotions and relationships. When the going gets tough, he walks away. Kassie never did experience any real abuse from mum although she did meet Uncle Joe. I don't know how far that went, because we don't talk about it. She was too young to remember the rest of us getting abused.

Kassie is the only one who still speaks to mum and none of the other kids speak to Kassie much. We were all jealous of her and how special she was treated. She still defends mum even though she knows better.

I speak to Kassie on the computer occasionally as she looks after Molly's son. She tries to understand but it is hard for her. She has food issues and is morbidly obese.

Molly--rest in peace Molly--one day your son will know how much you loved him and learn the truth that you couldn't live with your demons.

Then finally me, Abbie. I am the lucky one. I came out swinging, fought battle after battle and managed by some miracle to survive. I found true love and a man who helped me deal with my demons. He helped me learn to love and to trust. It took a lot of years and I do still struggle at times. But at least I have a loving family, a support system to help me forget my nightmares and hold my head up high having some pride in my victory.

Since Lilly was born, our families came to understood that Lawrie and I were an item in for the long haul. Maggie and I became the best of friends. She is my mum and is always there for me when I need her. I'm so sorry I put her through all the hell I did, it wasn't personal. Maggie's boys never forgave her for leaving them with their dad. They never understood she did it out of love and haven't really spoken to her since.

I don't work anymore--What am I saying?--but Lawrie and I foster children in care. There are still so many children with stories like mine, and they are just as angry as I was. But everyone needs someone to love and we try to do our part.

I have been living with Lawrie for 26 years and married for 22. No it hasn't all been plain sailing, no relationship is, but we are still together and that's more than a lot of "normal" people can say. Without a strong will to survive and the love of Lawrie and our girls, I probably wouldn't be here to write this story. In the end I just want to tell you one thing: It's okay to cry. Never ever give up hope! One day someone WILL see your invisible tears.

Lightning Source UK Ltd.
Milton Keynes UK
23 April 2010

153209UK00001B/9/P